Wine Tour

NAPA VALLEY

Jeffrey Caldewey

A Vintage Image Book

Published by The Wine Appreciation Guild

Other Books Published by THE WINE APPRECIATION GUILD:
THE CHAMPAGNE COOKBOOK
EPICUREAN RECIPES OF CALIFORNIA WINEMAKERS
GOURMET WINE COOKING THE EASY WAY
FAVORITE RECIPES OF CALIFORNIA WINEMAKERS
DINNER MENUS WITH WINE
EASY RECIPES OF CALIFORNIA WINEMAKERS
THE POCKET ENCYCLOPEDIA OF CALIFORNIA WINE
WINE LOVERS COOKBOOK
IN CELEBRATION OF WINE AND LIFE
WINE CELLAR RECORD BOOK
CORKSCREWS: An Introduction to Their Appreciation
THE CALIFORNIA WINE DRINK BOOK
THE CALIFORNIA BRANDY DRINK BOOK
NEW ADVENTURES IN WINE COOKERY
WINE IN EVERYDAY COOKING
THE VINTAGE IMAGE SERIES:
THE NAPA VALLEY WINE BOOK
THE SONOMA MENDOCINO TOUR BOOK
THE SOMOMA MENDOCINO WINE BOOK
THE CENTRAL COAST TOUR BOOK
THE CENTRAL COAST WINE BOOK
VINTAGEWISE
POCKET ENCYCLOPEDIA OF AMERICAN WINE, East of the Rockies

PUBLISHED BY:
The Wine Appreciation Guild
155 Connecticut Street
San Francisco, CA 94107
(415) 864-1202 / (800) 231-WINE

RESEARCH AND PRODUCTION: RONNA NELSON
AUTHOR: JEFFREY CALDEWEY

LIBRARY OF CONGRESS Cataloging in Publication Data

Wine Tour.

  "A Vintage Image Book."
  Previous publications classified separately and analyzed.
  Contents: [v. 1] Napa Valley / Jeffrey Caldewey.
  1. Wine and wine making — California — Napa River Valley — Collected works. 2. Napa River Valley (Calif.) —
Description and travel — Collected works. I. Caldewey, Jeffrey.
TP557.W693 1984   917.94'19'0453   84-10390
ISBN 0-932664-31-8 (v. 1)

PRINTED IN THE UNITED STATES OF AMERICA

Table of Contents

LOWER VALLEY WINERIES MAP   6-7
UPPER VALLEY WINERIES MAP   8-9
NAPA CITY MAP   11
YOUNTVILLE TOWN MAP   13
ST. HELENA TOWN MAP   15
CALISTOGA TOWN MAP   17
FOOD-reviews of restaurants and provenders,
    geographically listed south to north   18
RESTAURANT MENUS - the vintners' choice   35
LODGING - reviews of lodgings and accommodations,
    geographically listed south to north   47
WINERY INDEX - vital winemaking and visitor information,
    alphabetically listed   60
ADVENTURES - picnic areas & campgrounds,
    sightseeing possibilities, wine
    touring services, etc.   88

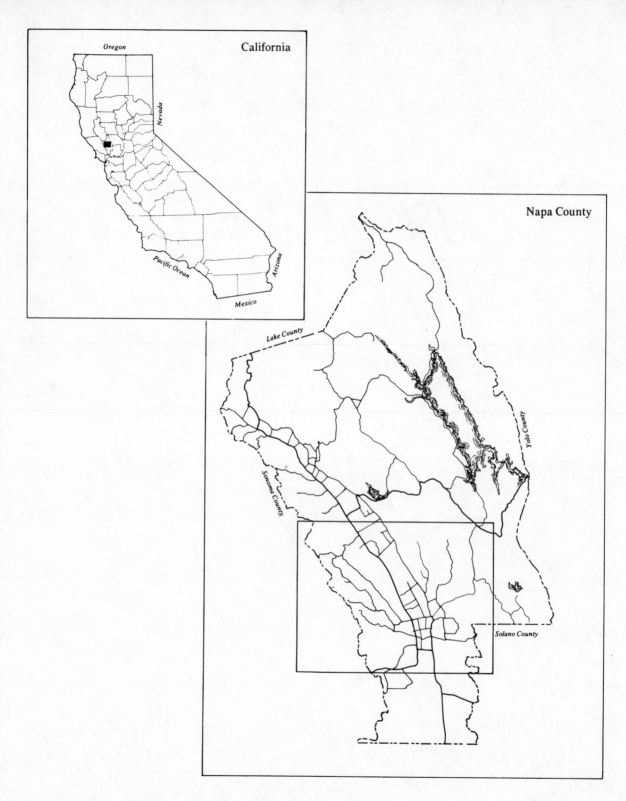

California

Oregon

Nevada

Pacific Ocean

Arizona

Mexico

Napa County

Lake County

Yolo County

Sonoma County

Solano County

6

CAKEBREAD CELLARS
JOHNSON TURNBULL VINEYARDS ■ EVENSON VINEYARDS
ROBERT MONDAVI WINERY ■ SILVER OAK CELLARS

Rector Reservoir

Atlas Peak 2663'

Cross
OAKVILLE
Oakville Grade
■ VICHON ■ ROBERT PEPI
FAR NIENTE ■
NAPA WINE CELLARS ■

Oakville Cross Rd.
■ S. ANDERSON VINEYARD
■ SILVERADO VYDS.
■ PINE RIDGE

Yount Mill Rd.
Yountville Cross Rd.

■ SHAFER VINEYARDS

DOMAINE CHANDON ■
CHATEAU CHEVRE WINERY ■
★ YOUNTVILLE

■ STAGS' LEAP WINERY
■ STAG'S LEAP WINE CELLARS

Atlas Peak Rd.

29

Trinity Rd.
VOSE VINEYARDS ■

LAKESPRING ■

Silverado Trail

■ CLOS DU VAL

Soda Canyon Rd.

★ GLEN ELLEN
Mt. Veeder 2677'
■ MAYACAMAS VINEYARDS
SKY VINEYARDS ■
Lokoya Rd.

NEWLAN ■
Darms

■ TREFETHEN VINEYARDS

121

MT. VEEDER WINERY ■
Mt. Veeder Rd.

Orchard Ave.
Oak Knoll Ave.
Salvador Ave.
Big Ranch Rd.
Hardman

Sleeping Elephant Mtn.
1753'

Dry Creek Rd.
ST. ANDREW'S ■
■ JOHN BECKETT CELLARS

Napa County
Sonoma County
MONT LA SALLE ■
Partrick Rd.
Redwood Rd.

Truncas St.
Monticello Rd.
1st Ave.

3rd Ave.

Sonoma Hwy.
DON CHARLES ROSS ■
Lincoln Ave.

Soscol

County

Browns Valley Rd.
Buhman
1st St.

■ TULOCAY WINERY
Coombsville Rd.

SONOMA ★
Lovell Valley Rd.
Buena Vista Rd.
Napa Rd.
Henry Rd.

NAPA ★
Jefferson
3rd
Imola
■ WILLIAM HILL WINERY

Miliken Peak 743'
CARNEROS CREEK WINERY ■
Deaby Ln.
Old Sonoma Rd.
■ MONT ST. JOHN

Napa River

12
121

Cuttings Wharf

12
29

■ ACACIA

■ CHATEAU BOUCHAINE

Napa Valley South

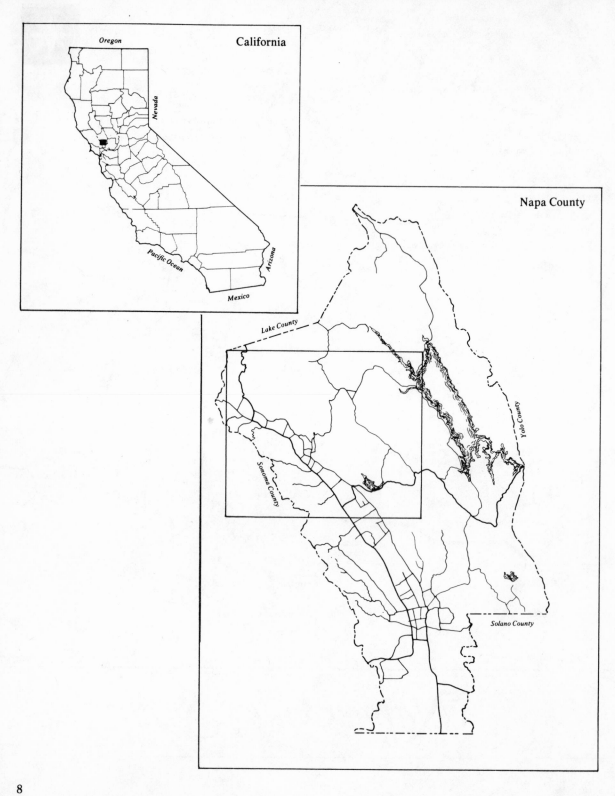

California

Oregon

Nevada

Pacific Ocean

Arizona

Mexico

Napa County

Lake County

Yolo County

Sonoma County

Solano County

8

STORYBOOK MOUNTAIN VINEYARDS
PECOTA WINERY
CHATEAU MONTELENA

TRAULSEN

CALISTOGA
CUVAISON
STERLING
STONEGATE

RODDIS CELLAR
DIAMOND CREEK VINEYARDS
SCHRAMSBERG VINEYARDS
ALTA VINEYARD CELLAR
STONY HILL VINEYARD

Evey Rd.
Tubbs Lane
Lincoln Ave.
Calistoga Airport
Dunaweal
Diamond Mtn. Rd.
St. Helena Hwy.
Bothe-Napa State Park
Larkmead
Bale
Crystal Springs

CHATEAU BOSWELL
HANNS KORNELL CHAMPAGNE CELLARS
BURGESS CELLARS
CHARLES F. SHAW WINERY
TUDAL WINERY
FROG'S LEAP

RITCHIE CREEK VINEYARD
SMITH-MADRONE VINEYARDS
FREEMARK ABBEY WINERY
ROBERT KEENAN
YVERDON VINEYARDS
ST. CLEMENT VINEYARDS
CHATEAU CHEVALIER WINERY
CHRISTIAN BROTHERS
SPRING MOUNTAIN WINERY
BERINGER WINERY

St. Helena Rd.

ST. HELENA WINE CO.

CASA NUESTRA
DUCKHORN VINEYARDS
ROUND HILL WINERY
MARKHAM WINERY
CHARLES KRUG WINERY
CALAFIA

Zinfandel

DEER PARK WINERY

Deer Park Rd.
Howell Mtn. Rd.
Conn Valley Rd.

DUNN VYDS

ANGWIN

POPE VALLEY WINERY

POPE VALLEY

White Cottage Rd.
Ink Grade
Pope Valley Rd.
Pope Canyon Rd.
Hardin Rd.

GREEN AND RED VINEYARD

BUEHLER VINEYARDS

Greenfield Rd.
Chiles Pope Valley Rd.
Lower Chiles Valley Rd.

NICHELINI VINEYAR

Lodi

29

Pratt
Pope St.

St. Helena Rd.
Spring Mtn. Rd.

ST. HELENA

NAPA CREEK WINERY
JOSEPH PHELPS VINEYARDS
HEITZ WINE CELLARS

Taplin

128

RUTHERFORD HILL WINERY

Lake Hennessey
Sage Canyon Rd.

CHAPPELLET VINEYARDS
LONG VINEYARDS

PRAGER WINERY & PORT WORKS
SUTTER HOME WINERY
V. SATTUI WINERY

White Sulphur Springs Rd.

LOUIS MARTINI
HEITZ TASTING

RAYMOND
SULLIVAN
CONN CREEK WINERY

Napa County

Sonoma County

Sonoma Hwy.

FLORA SPRINGS WINE CO.
FRANCISCAN VINEYARDS
RUTHERFORD VINTNERS
GRGICH HILLS CELLARS

Mt. St. John 2375

INGLENOOK VINEYARDS

NIEBAUM-COPPOLA ESTATES

Whitehall
Niebaum Lane
Manly Ln.

SHOWN & SONS
Z. D. WINERY
WHITEHALL LANE WINERY
SEQUOIA GROVE
BEAULIEU VINEYARD

CAYMUS VINEYARDS

RUTHERFORD

VILLA MT. EDEN
CASSAYRE-FORNI CELLARS

OAKVILLE

Silverado Trail
Oakville Cross

GIRARD WINERY

Napa Valley North

CITY OF NAPA
PERSPECTIVE

The name Napa is a corruption of the Indian word "Nappa," as the natives at the mouth of the river called their settlement. When pioneer George Yount came here in 1831, he estimated there were between ten and twelve thousand Indians living in the Napa Valley. They lived peacefully but they possessed the universal trait of being unable to adapt to the ways of the invading white men. In 1833, cholera broke out and thousands of Indians died. Within a decade the Indian population of Napa Valley was decimated.

In 1845, a group of Californians, which later became known as "The Bear Flag Party," gathered in the nearby town of Sonoma to declare California's independence from Mexico. Two years later a member of this group, Nathan Coombs, surveyed the original town site of Napa. The city's first building was erected in 1848, but before its completion news of the discovery of gold reached owner Harrison Pierce causing him to abandon the project to try his luck in the gold fields. Pierce returned later that year disilluisioned by his failure to find sudden riches and opened "The Empire Saloon."

Simpson Thomas planted the first European grape cuttings in 1852 on their Soscol land grant south of Napa city. Pioneer vintner Charles Krug produced the first European style wine in the Napa region on the ranch of John Patchett in 1858. The wine industry of Napa Valley flourished partially as a result of Napa city's location on the navigational head of Napa River. Schooners plied her waters as early as 1841 and a steamship line to San Francisco was established in 1850, providing inexpensive and reliable transportation to the metropolitan market place. The valley opened like a cornucopia at the city of Napa which controlled the region's trade for almost a century.

With the advent of motor trucking systems, Napa lost its usefulness as the valley's market place. Commuting workers from nearby industrial centers have helped to quadruple the city's population since the end of World War II, precipitating the subsequent suburban sprawl. During the past ten years, growth in the guise of progress has devastated this one-time Victorian gem, and it has only been very recently that the local populace has made any attempt to rescue its history from the wrecker's ball.

A drive through the downtown residential section will reward the visitor with a glimpse of Napa's glorious past, with many fine examples of 19th Century architecture. Fuller Park, bounded by Oak and Jefferson streets, is a pleasant tree-shaded siesta or picnic stop. The old Tulocay Cemetery on the east side of the river is the final resting place for many of Napa's citizens, both illustrious and notorious, including Mammy Pleasant, infamous madame and voodoo queen.

Two of Napa's famous ranches have been transformed into resorts. On the northern outskirts of town is the Silverado Country Club, originally the home of Civil War General John Miller and now a twelve-hundred acre resort complete with golf courses, tennis courts, five swimming pools, and 190 guest rooms. A drive out Coombsville Road (named after the city's founder) winds through a majestic valley and ends at Wild Horse Valley Ranch, a three-thousand acre horse riding estate.

Napa

CITY OF YOUNTVILLE
PERSPECTIVE

The first American to settle in the Napa Valley was George Yount, a representative pioneer, soldier, hunter, trapper, frontiersman, who came overland from North Carolina in 1831. Because he traveled the entire breadth of the continent, Yount was linked with many early events in the American occupation of the West.

Toward the end of 1833, Yount visited the Mexican missions in San Rafael and Sonoma and made the acquaintance of Mariano Guadalupe Vallejo, Commandante General of Alta California. Vallejo admired the ingenuity and resourcefulness of the intrepid pioneer and the two became lifelong friends. In 1835, Yount became a Mexican citizen and converted to Catholicism, baptized Jorge Concepcion Yount. As a reward for his loyalty and service, he was given a land grant consisting of 11,814 acres lying in the heart of Napa Valley. The "Caymus Land Grant" was the first is Napa county and Yount's dwelling was the area's first wooden structure.

Yount understood and respected Indians, at least to the extent that he was able to utilize their labor to his advantage without undue coercion. With their help, he planted vineyards, and took the grapes to Vallejo's winery. He aslo raised cattle and sheep, maintained fruit orchards, and built both a sawmill and a flour mill.

Rancho Caymus became a regular stopping place for immigrant parties. Yount greeted newcomers hospitably, let them camp near his home, gave them advice on where they could settle, and assisted them in exchanging their skilled workmanship for land. His friendliness, however, was ill-requited. After the Land Act of 1851 threw titles of existing Mexican land grant holders into confusion, squatters overran the valley. They took possession of Yount's land where they could and caused more trouble, according to Yount, than Indians and grizzly bears combined.

By 1855, a bustling village had grown on the southern border of Rancho Caymus consisting of two hotels, a blacksmith shop and two stores. After Yount's death at age seventy-one, the town's name was changed from Sebastopol to Yountville in his honor.

George Yount's gravesite is in the cemetery at the corner of Jackson and Washington Streets and is registered as a California State Historical Landmark. Part of the cemetery has, since its formation in 1848, been reserved for Indian burial grounds. Interred on this spot are the ashes of the local Wappo Indian tribes. On adjoining property is Yountville's city park, which provides convenient off-the-road picnic facilities.

A trip to Yountville is not complete without a visit to Vintage 1870. This two-story shopping complex was once the proud winemaking domain of Gottlieb Groezinger. Today quaint shops on the premises offer everything from gourmet foods and wine to crafts, clothing and antiques. One of the most unusual and spectacular sights here is the launching of a hot-air balloon manned by local aeronaut Steve Frattini. Reservations can be made for champagne flights aboard his multi-colored balloon, providing a truly heavenly view of Napa Valley.

Yountville

CITY OF ST. HELENA
PERSPECTIVE

Edward Bale, an impoverished English surgeon, came to California aboard a whaling ship in 1834. He jumped ship in Monterey where he began medical practice. As surgeon to the Mexican forces, he met and later married General Vallejo's niece and subsequently became a naturalized Mexican citizen. In 1839, he was given title to the Carna Humana Rancho, a land grant that comprised all of northern Napa Valley, including what is now Calistoga and St. Helena. The entire property consisted of almost twenty thousand acres of virgin land.

In 1846, because of the demand for flour, Dr. Bale built a mill on a creekside location three miles north of the present site of St. Helena. Grist and flour were produced here for the next thirty years. The Old Bale Mill today has been completely restored and is a State of California Registered Historical Landmark.

In 1853, another Englishman, J.H. Still, purchased one hundred acres of property from the Bale estate and opened a general store. Two years later, Mr. Still, anxious to see a town started, offered to donate land to those who wanted to engage in business. By 1858, St. Helena was a flourishing town, complete with shoe shop, hotel, mercantile store, wagon shop, and, of course, the ubiquitous saloon. There is some dispute as to how the town actually received its name, but there seems little doubt the name was suggested by the fact that Mount St. Helena stands as a sentinel at the head of the Napa Valley.

Travelers journey north from the lower region of Napa to reach St. Helena at the very heart of the wine country. It is still a quaint Victorian village, little changed since the eighteen hundreds. Population has increased by scarcely a thousand souls in the last century, accounting for the pastoral quality of life in St. Helena.

St. Helena is the home of several institutions unique to the valley's winemaking industry. In the Richie Building, an ornate three-story architectural landmark built in 1896, are the studios of renowned designers Colonna, Caldewey and Farrell.

Several blocks away, off Adams Street, is the Napa Valley Wine Library. Here is housed one of America's largest collections of wine-related books with rare and arcane volumes from all the enological regions of the world. Summer wine appreciation courses sponsored by the library offer an in-depth sensory evaluation experience.

On the outskirts of town, down Lodi Lane, visitors can see coopers assembling oak casks in the time-honored tradition. The Barrel Builders firm provides wood cooperage for many of California's vintners and also manufactures the increasingly popular ''hot tub'' used for Japanese-style outdoor bathing.

St. Helena boasts two idyllic parks for picnickers. Crane park, located at the end of Grayson Ave. behind the high school, is an isolated 5-acre site with tennis courts, baseball fields, playground and restrooms. There are a dozen oak-shaded picnic tables complete with barbecues. Four miles north of town is Bothe-Napa Valley State Park. Dozens of picnic tables dot the 1242-acre park.

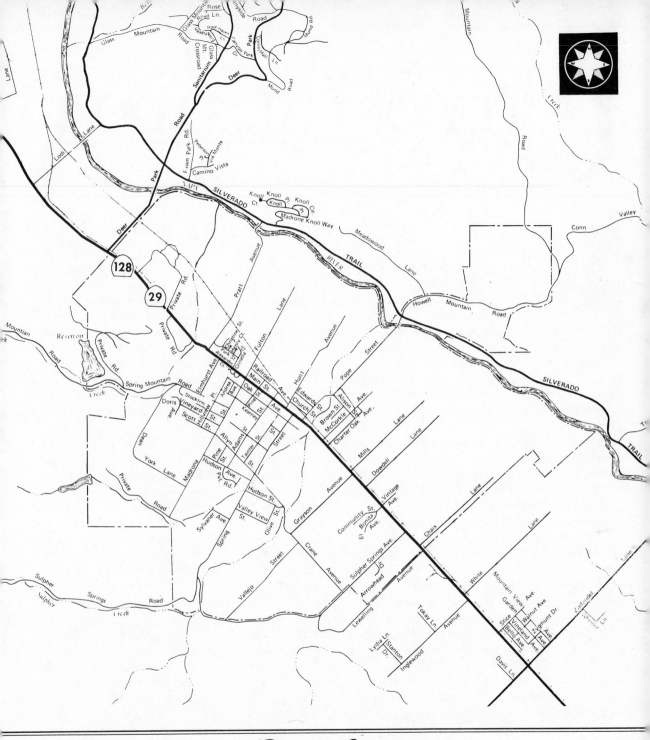

St. Helena

CITY OF CALISTOGA
PERSPECTIVE

The Indians were intuitively aware of the great medicinal value of Napa Valley's mineral springs. They wore trails through the densely wooded hills and valley floor making their regular pilgrimages to bathe in the health-giving waters. The first English speaking settlers here established a community which they called simply "Hot Springs," but the epithet "Calistoga" was coined by the near legendary California pioneer Sam Brannan.

Sam Brannan was twenty-seven years old in 1846 when he brought a shipload of Mormons from New York to Yerba Buena (now San Francisco). He subsequently established California's first newspaper and was the first to print word of the discovery of gold in 1848. During the gold rush, Brannan operated the only store in the entire Sacramento Valley. He subsequently became California's first banker, first land developer and first millionaire.

Beginning 1859, Brannan acquired more than two-thousand acres at the foot of Mt. St. Helena. It was his intention to establish the greatest resort spa in the West—a challenge which he pursued with great zeal, risking and eventually losing his entire fortune.

During 1860, the lavish main hotel and 25 guest cottages were built. The original general store at the corner of Wapoo Street is now dedicated with an historical marker. One of the guest cottages now stands across from the city hall and has been restored by the Napa County Historical Society. The resort had an observatory where guests could get an aerial view of the entire countryside. It had many other special attractions: race track, golf course, swimming pool, mud and sulphur baths, skating rink, winery and distillery.

By 1872, Brannan had outspent his fortune. Hopelessly over-extended, he lost his interest in the resort and it was auctioned off piecemeal. Sam Brannan died penniless 20 years later.

Today there are six spas in Calistoga offering the same healthful hot mineral waters, steam and mud baths that made this area famous. Calistoga's Old Faithful Geyser, one of three such natural phenomena in the world, still erupts from the earth at periodic intervals. Some of the hoopla that attended Brannan's extravagant days in Calistoga returns each year at the Napa County Fair held the first week of July.

To Calistoga visitors, a breathtaking view of the whole Napa Valley is available from the cockpit of a glider. The engineless craft are towed aloft from the airport located on Lincoln Avenue to altitudes of several thousand feet. Tremendous updrafts created by the surrounding mountain ranges can keep the planes soaring for hours.

A similarly awesome view awaits the more earth-bound traveler who takes the trip to Robert Lewis Stevenson Park atop Mount St. Helena, The famous author honeymooned here in 1880, and a plaque marks the spot where the newlyweds' cabin stood. A five-mile hiking trail leads from the park to the top of Mount St. Helena (elevation 4500 feet).

Pioneer Park, located in downtown Calistoga at the Corner of Spring and Cedar Streets, offers visitors a quiet creekside picnic setting.

Calistoga

Food

 he charming rural region of Napa Valley has a very provincial air which is in marked contrast to the cosmopolitan urban centers only an hour and a half away. It is sometimes assumed by sophisticated visitors that the only way to stave off starvation while touring the wine country is to pack a picnic lunch and then hurry home to dinner. There are, however, a surprising number of very good roadside bistros and eateries to be found secluded in this famous vineyard community. After all, the well-developed palates of the local populace cannot be sated by wine alone!

The intention of this guide is to help wine travelers looking for a good restaurant by providing them with a list of establishments which are in some way noteworthy.

A consensus of winery spokespeople and local restaurateurs initially compiled the list of restaurants selected for review. Restaurants have been carefully evaluated for freshness and quality of food, service, atmosphere and price range. No effort has been made to formally classify these restaurants; rather, the intent has been to inform the traveler of what is expected when visiting them.

For those interested in a picnic lunch among the vines, a listing of shops purveying provisions is included, as well as the wine shops which specialize in often hard-to-get local wines. Wine shop proprietors, not surprisingly, are often the most knowledgeable sources of newsworthy vineyard gossip and are usually more than willing to offer a well-informed opinion of the latest releases.

Travel Notes: _____

_____

_____

THE CURB SIDE CAFE   *Restaurant*

Napa Valley's ''other'' breakfast spot, the Curbside Cafe, specializes in robust country style breakfasts. Portions are so large they border on the ridiculous. Huge mounds of pan fried new potatoes are served up with bulging, three egg omelettes stuffed with asparagus, bacon, tomato and cheddar cheese, along with several slices of hot, buttery wheatberry bread all for $3.95. (It is no exaggeration to suggest splitting this breakfast between two people.)

For something a little lighter to start the day, try the continental, fresh fruit and made from scratch their spicy apple nut bread ($1.95).

The appropriately named Curbside Cafe is located in the heart of downtown Napa. Two walls of glass provide a view of bustling Napkins (the local slang for residents of Napa City). Inside, the scene is bustling as well. Nearly touching tables provide cozy seating for fifty tightly packed patrons.

The Curbside Cafe, 1245 First St., Napa 94558. Telephone (707) 253-2307. Hours: Mon. - Sat. 7 a.m. - 4 p.m. Thurs. evening 5 - 8 p.m. Price range: breakfast: $1.45 - $5.00. Lunch $1.95 - $5.25. No cards.

NUNN'S CHEESE BARN — *Provisions*

This quaint little establishment has existed on the present location in one form or another for over one hundred and fifteen years. Originally a stage coach stop — now Nunn's houses a delicatessen featuring over 120 cheeses from around the world. They boast a huge selection of cold cuts and homemade salads. Fresh bagettes of bread are delivered Wednesday-Saturday from the renowned Sonoma French Bakery. Also available is a large selection of beer and wine. Customers may dine on the garden terrace covered by a 100 year old wisteria vine.

Nunn's Cheese Barn, 1427 Main St., Napa 94558. Telephone (707) 255-0262. Hours: Mon. - Tues. 10:00 a.m. 5:00 p.m. Wed. - Sat. 10:00 a.m. - 6:00 p.m. No Cards.

ANDREWS MEAT COMPANY — *Provisions*

Napa's old main street section is being resurrected from the wrecker's ball. The stone Pfieffer Brewery Building, originally constructed in 1875, now houses the Andrews Meat Company. This family run operation offers high quality meats, cold cuts, and cheeses. Sandwiches are available for picnics ($1.50 - $2.85) or may be consumed on the premises in the spacious 2nd story dining room or on the sunny outdoor deck. A limited selection of beer and wine is available and a well stocked salad bar is offered.

Andrews Meat Company, 1245 Main St., Napa 94558. Telephone (707) 253-8311. Hours: 8 a.m. - 6 p.m. Mon. - Fri. Sat. 8 a.m. - 5:30 p.m. Closed Sunday. No Cards. Seating 100.

THE DINER   *Restaurant*

Owners Nicki Hamilton and Cassandra Mitchell make it all seem so simple. Down-home quality food, prepared fresh, cooked properly and at reasonable prices. The truth is, creating a great restaurant requires a great deal of skill and perseverance and only the most accomplished restaurateurs make it seem effortless.

Many locals consider the Diner in Yountville to be the only good place in the Napa Valley to eat breakfast, and with good reason. The menu ranges from the traditional bacon and eggs to avocado and sour cream omelettes to Mexican omelettes with cheese, olives, tomatoes, and chile sauce, all generously served with grilled potatoes and toasted sourdough French bread. For a slight extra charge, get the seasoned potatoes; they are worth it.

The lunch menu features a dozen different hot and cold sandwiches and such specialties as the Humdinger — a charbroiled cheeseburger on a grilled English muffin with lettuce, onions and French fries. Different soups and luncheon specials are prepared daily.

The dinner menu offers a unique array of south of the border specialty dishes such as chicken mole and broiled fish veracruzana salsa. Both imported and domestic beer is available.

The Diner, 6476 Washington St., Yountville 94599. Telephone (707) 944-2626. Hours: Tues.-Sun. 8 a.m. - 3 p.m. Dinner Thurs. - Sun. 6:00 - 9:30. Price range: Breakfast, $1.50-$4.50; Lunch, $2.00-$4.50; Dinner, $4.25-$8.00. Seating: 40.

Travel Notes: _____

_____

_____

DOMAINE CHANDON   *Restaurant*

The restaurant at Domaine Chandon is meant to be a showcase of their sparkling wines. The setting is an elegant architectural jewel of wood and glass, an elegant island in a sea of vines. The restaurant presents a three course luncheon featuring soup (try the splendid cream of tomato, baked in a puffed pastry shell), charcuterie, and superb pastries. Two different entrees change on a weekly basis.

During the warm months guests can dine in one of the most private and bucolic outdoor settings in the valley where an atmosphere of gaiety always prevails. Be sure to allow at least two hours for luncheon.

Dinners are given a more refined treatment. The service, while still leisurely, is more formal, The Menu is extremely ambitious and occasionally overreaches itself. The pate stuffed quail is a perfect appetizer. The entrees are weighted towards "Fruits de mer". The cassoulet of fresh fish and crustaceans is served with a light champagne cream sauce. The desserts are always memorable.

The restaurant now offers more than an adequate selection of Napa Valley wines. The salon is open for sparkling winetasting by the glass or bottle.

Domaine Chandon, California Drive, Yountville 94599. Telephone (707) 944-2892. Hours: Lunch, 11:30 - 2:30 Daily. Dinner: 6:00 - 9:00 Wed. - Sun. Salon: 11:00 a.m. - 6:00 p.m. daily. Closed Mon. and Tues. in Winter. Price range: Lunch, $20.00; Complete Dinner, $40.00; Corkage, $3.00. Suggest two week advance reservation. Cards: AE, VISA, MC.

THE FRENCH LAUNDRY   *Restaurant*

This stone and redwood structure originally a turn of the century French Laundry has been transformed into an elegant restaurant setting. The Schmitt family home is adjacent to the restaurant's luxuriant herb and flower gardens and lends emphasis to the fact that this is entirely a family effort with Sally, Don and their five children all involved in the preparation and service of the memorable cuisine. Long-time residents will remember Sally's hand at the helm of the original Chutney Kitchen at Vintage 1870.

The menu, usually prepared in French country style, is dictated by the availablity of fresh produce and seasonal meats and fish; a single entree is offered nightly. Meals are prepared simply and attractively served, and come with a rich soup du jour and refreshing fresh green salad. There is always a choice of appetizers and desserts as well as good cheeses all on a la carte basis.

The French Laundry delights the eye as well as the palate, with tasteful decor, fresh cut flowers, and relaxed, friendly ambiance—Sally won't mind if you peek into her beautifully homey kitchen.

The wine list is well selected and features a number of small local wineries, all priced $2.00 over retail. They also offer a fine selection of older wines, reasonably priced.

The French Laundry, Corner of Washington & Creek St., Yountville 94599. Telephone (707) 944-2380. Hours: Dinner only, Wednesday through Sunday. Price range: complete dinners from $30.00. Corkage $5.00. No Cards. Reservations and confirmations are required.

Travel Notes: _____

_____

_____

MAMA NINA'S   *Restaurant*

Fresh pastas are prepared daily at Mama Nina's and include lucious rings of Tortellini filled with ground veal and chicken, homemade Pesto and the specialty of the house, Fettuccini all' Alfredo.

Meals may be ordered a la carte, as a small dinner with soup or salad, or as a full dinner with antipasto tray, soup, salad, dessert and coffee. The meals are all served at a relaxed pace. One of the nicest features of Mama Nina's is the fact that they are open both Mondays and Tuesdays contrary to Napa Valley restaurant custom.

The soup of the day, usually a variation of minestrone, succeeds in being both full-bodied and delicately balanced. The salads of spinach, a combination of mixed greens, and a profusion of walnuts and mushroom slices are attractively presented.

Entrees feature a delightful Veal Piccata prepared with Lemon and capers; chicken in wine and mushrooms, and Scampi in butter, olive oil, garlic and wine. Also offered nightly are Italian specialties such as Canneloni, Osso Buco and a hearty veal stew.

The wine list has a selection limited to Napa valley and Sonoma wineries. Mama Nina's has one of the most sociable bars in the lower valley with ample seating, cordial bartenders, and a cheery fireplace.

Mama Nina's, 6772 Washington St., Yountville 94599. Telephone (707) 944-2112. Hours: on season, seven days a week, 11:30 a.m. - 2:30 p.m., 5:00 p.m. - 10:00 p.m., off season, closed Wednesdays. Price range: $4.95 - $11.95. Reservations suggested. Cards: VISA, MC. Seating capacity 130. Upstairs banquet facility available.

MUSTARDS GRILL   *Restaurant*

Located just north of Yountville is Napa Valley's new and highly acclaimed Mustards Grill. Masterminded by Chef Cindy Pawylsen and her three partners, Mustards offers unique dishes such as roast garlic and Sonoma rabbit. The atmosphere is comfortable and relaxed with white table cloths and potted palms. You will frequently find Robert Mondavi and other winemakers and celebreties there.

Accompanying the menu are three to seven addi-

tional specials including fresh fish usually prepared on the mesquite grill. (The mesquite is direct from Mexico and is supplied to other restaurants by Mustards). You will find foods with an Oriental, Italian, and Continental flare attributed to the internationally traveled chef. Many of the American dishes; smoked lemon chicken, barbequed back ribs and smoked pork loin with apple lemon sauce and black beans are prepared in the oakwood burning oven. Sandwiches are also available.

A selective wine list changes every six weeks, premium wines are available by the glass. Vingtage Port and Apperitifs always available.

Mustards Grill, 7399 St. Helena Highway, Yountville. Reservations advised. Telephone (707) 944-2424. Hours: Lunch 11:30 - 3:00, Dinner 5:00 - 10:00 daily. Price Range: $5.00 to $12.00. Cards: VISA, MC. Seating Capacity: 82.

GROEZINGER WINE COMPANY   *Provisions*

Behind the brick shopping complex of Vintage 1870 stands the massive Groezinger Winery Stables, out of use since Prohibition. The building has been refurbished and now houses the appropriately named Groezinger Wine Company. Thousands of bottles culled from over one hundred fifty California wineries are attractively displayed on rough-hewn wooden shelves, as well as a representative sampling of one hundred imported wines. There is also a tasting bar.

Groezinger Wine Company, Vintage 1870, Yountville 94599. Telephone (707) 944-2331. Hours: 10:00 a.m. - 5:30 p.m. daily. Cards: VISA, MC.

VINTAGE 1870 *Provisions*

The Vintage 1870 shopping complex houses two stores which purvey supplies for picnics. The Thrifty Gourmet contains a small delicatessen where several dozen cheeses, cold meats, French bread and bagels are available for sandwich fixings. No alcoholic beverages are availabe here, but new owners Susan and Albert Clymer, locals (Yountville) stock numerous organic juices including apple-strawberry and black cherry. Adjacent to the deli is a gourmet section where customers can find imported teas, tins and boxes of crackers, herbs, spices, jams and other delicacies. The Thrifty Gourmet's own brand of coffee is ground to order.

Tom and Nancy Catterson's shop is facetiously called The Wurst Place in the Napa Valley. They claim to have Northern California's largest assortment of sausages, as well as other quality meats. The Wurst Place stocks everything from pheasant and fresh rabbit to home-made Polish Kielbasa. Casings and spices for do-it-yourself sausage makers are also available.

For the barbecue, they offer excellent, aged New York steaks and meaty pork loin back ribs.

The Thrifty Gourmet, Vintage 1870, Yountville 94599. Telephone (707) 944-8100. Hours: 10:00 a.m. - 5:30 p.m. Daily. Cards: VISA, MC.

The Wurst Place, Vintage 1870, Yountville 94599. Telephone (707) 944-2224. Hours: 10:00 a.m. - 5:00 p.m., Tues. - Sun. No Cards.

VINTAGE 1870 *Restaurant, Bar*

The massive complex called Vintage 1870 was once the winemaking domain of Gottlieb Groezinger. Prohibition brought his enterprise to an untimely end, and the structure now houses a myriad of unique shops.

At the Chutney Kitchen, fresh salads and home-made soups are the specialties. Sandwiches include turkey, avocado and cream cheese, baked ham and smoked tongue. For dessert, the cheesecake is excellent. Antiques, bentwood chairs and flowered quilt tablecloths provide a country ambiance. Seating is also available on the secluded outside patio, spring and summer.

The Vintage Cafe is housed in the old railroad station on the property. An outdoor deck facing the entrance of Vintage 1870 provides the perfect location for people-watching while imbibing a cold Heineken beer. The Vintage Cafe specializes in delicious charcoal-broiled hamburgers (considered by many to be the best in Napa Valley) served on a toasted French roll with a fresh green salad. The espresso machine churns out some enlivening coffee drinks such as Mocha Cafe.

The Chutney Kitchen, Vintage 1870, Yountville 94599. Telephone (707) 944-2788. Hours: Mon. - Fri. 12:00 - 3:00 p.m. Sat., Sun., 11:30 - 4:00. Price range: $1.50 - $4.95. Cards: VISA, MC. Seating 85.

The Vintage Cafe, Vintage 1870, Yountville 94599. Telephone (707) 944-2614. Hours: 10:00 a.m. - 5:00 p.m. Mon. - Fri., 10:00 a.m. - 6:00 p.m. Sat. - Sun. Price range: $1.50 - $4.75. Seating 100.

Travel Notes: _____

_____

_____

LE CHARDONNAY   *Restaurant*

Le Chardonnay is located in an absolutely charming little brick building on Yountville's Restaurant Row. ''Maitre d' '' Philippe Ouali simply bubbles over with gallic charm, while his partner, Bernard Moutal presides over the kitchen. The cuisine is French, but with a heavy hand - plenty of spices, heavy sauces and large portions - lovers of Nouvelle Cuisine be warned! The menu has several innovative offerings such as salmon en croute and scallops in ginger sauce, but at a price that rivals the most expensive restaurants in the valley. Lunch offers a better value. In spite of its name, Le Chardonnay's wine list is somewhat limited.

Le Chardonnay, 6534 Washington St., Yountville 94599. Telephone (707) 944-2521. Hours: closed Monday. Lunch 11:30 - 2:30, Dinner 6:00 - 10:30. Price range: $14.75 - $19.75. Seating: 40 people.

WASHINGTON STREET   *Restaurant, Bar*

100 years north of Vintage 1870 stands the old Gottlieb Groezinger residence. Flanked by century-old palm trees, the thoughtfully-restored brick building has recently opened under the ownership of Rich and Tom Reed, brothers who originally hail from the Napa Valley. The freshly cooked food centers around a menu of steak, chops, lamb and seafood. The restaurant is open every day of the week and offers full bar service.

Washington Street Restuarant & Bar, 6539 Washington Street, Yountville 94599. Telephone (707) 944-2406. Hours: Dinner, every day 5:30 - 10:00, lunches, 11:30 - 2:30; Wednesday - Sunday. Price range $7.25 - $14.00. Corkage $4.00. MC, VISA. Seating 85.

Travel Notes: _____

_____

_____

25

OAKVILLE GROCERY CO. *Provisions, deli*

The Oakville Grocery Company, so lovingly put together by John and Pam Michels, is now owned by Joseph Phelps, of Phelps Winery fame. The store can be easily identified by the vintage 1930's Coca-Cola billboard on the side of the building. Once inside, a surprise awaits. Lining the shelves are tantalizing gourmet foods, imported cigarettes, dried fruit, imported beers, and local produce. Over two dozen meats and cheeses fill the deli case. This is the place to buy fresh sourdough French bread or have a sandwich made to order. The wine cellar stocks a number of wines from small local wineries. Recently, a new store bearing the Oakville Grocery Company banner has opened on San Francisco's Union Street.

Oakville Grocery Company, 7856 St. Helena Hwy., Oakville 94562. Telephone (707) 944-8802. Hours: daily, 10:00 a.m. - 6 p.m. VISA, MC.

AUBERGE DU SOLEIL *Restaurant, Inn*

Beyond the intersection of Silverado Trail and Rutherford Crossroad, looming several hundred feet above the valley floor, stands a new and exceedingly elegant restaurant. This impressive chateau-styled structure commands a spectacular view of the vineyards and wooded hills beyond. Indeed the restaurant's name derives from its western exposure; the setting sun viewed from the Veranda is an unforgetable sight.

Auberge du Soleil was conceived by Claus Rouas, owner of the much touted L'Etoile in San Francisco. As chef he enlisted equally renowned Masa Kobayashi. Although Masa has moved to his own new restaurant at the Vintage Court Hotel in San Francisco (which incidentally both the Hotel and Restaurant are achieving high acclaim in this sophisticated city), the Masa tradition of excellence is carried on by new chef Michel Cornu, previously of Aldophus of Dallas.

The prix fixe meal might consist of an exquisite al dente linguine studded with smoky truffles; a cream soup, perhaps reduced essence of scallops melded with cream and butter; entree, tender veal on a bed of spinach bathed in an aromatic morel sauce.

All is followed by a fresh green salad and an array of desserts.

The selection of wine at Auberge is extensive and expensive. Corkage is frowned upon.

Auburge du Soleil, 180 Rutherford Hill Road, Rutherford, CA Telephone (707) 963-1211. Open Thursday - Tuesday 6:00 - 10:00 p.m. Prix Fixe $36.00. Open for lunches 11:30 - 2:00. Cards: MC, VISA, AE. Seating: 65.

RUTHERFORD SQUARE   *Restaurant, Provisions*

Rutherford Square consists of the Cottage, a delicatessen; Corner Bar & Cellar, a cozy bar; the Garden Restaurant, a soup and luncheon eatery on the garden patio; and the Rutherford Square Theatre.

The delicatessen in the Cottage offers cheese and cold cuts, sandwiches ($2.25 - $2.75), homemade soup, crab and shrimp Louies, quiche, wines and cold imported beer. A weekend brunch with champagne omelettes is also available here. The deli in the cottage is open daily and features ice cream and espresso.

A stone's throw away is the Corner Bar & Cellar. This Lilliputian bar hold 15 people upstairs if a few of them stand. There is more room downstairs in the cellar with live music on weekends.

Homemade soup. salad and luncheon specialties are offered outdoors in the Garden Restaurant. This is a relaxed cafe type setting, one of the few in the Valley. Cocktails are available.

The Rutherford Square Theatre features dancing under the stars Sunday nights, July through September with Big Band sounds like Stan Kenton and Jimmy Dorsey and contemporary artists.

Rutherford Square, corner of Hwy. 29 and Rutherford Cross Rd., Box 500, Rutherford 94573. Telephone (707) 963-2617 and 963-2431. Hours: The Garden Restaurant (963-2617) 11:00 a.m. - 4:00 p.m. daily, May - Nov.; The Cottage (963-2317) 11:00 a.m. - 4 p.m. everyday; dinner, summer 6:30 - 9:00, Sat. - Tues.; Corner Bar, (963-7744) from 11 a.m.; Theatre, (963-2617) Sunday nights.

Travel Notes: _____

_____

_____

ERNIE'S WINE WAREHOUSE — *Provisions*

Owned by St. Helena resident Ernie Van Asperen of Ernie's liquor store fame, the Wine Warehouse features wines from around the world. On the shelves are several thousand bottles from France's Bordeaux and Burgundy regions. There are wines available from Australia, Italy, Germany and, of course, California.

Wines from the five dozen California wineries include those sold inexpensively under Ernie's private label. Ernie's Wine Warehouse places special emphasis on small California winery labels.

Ernies, 699 St. Helena Hwy., St. Helena 94574. Telephone (707) 963-7888. Hours: 10 a.m. - 6 p.m. daily. Cards: BA MC.

THE BOTTLE SHOP — *Provisions*

Fred Beringer, whose family operated the venerable Beringer Winery for three generations, is the proprietor of the Bottle Shop. Conveniently located on Main Street, the liquor store offers wines from many Napa Valley vintners as well as a selection from neighboring wine growing regions. This is the best place in St. Helena to stop for chilled wine or imported beer. Huge gold-framed lithographs of famous local wineries are attractively displayed from the walls.

The BottleShop, 1321 Main St., St. Helena 94574. Telephone (707) 963-3092. Hours: vary. Cards: VISA, MC, AMEX.

W.F. GIUGNI & SON — *Provisions, Deli*

Second generation owners Bill and Kathy Giugni have retained much of the original atmosphere of this friendly country store. Along with grocery items, Giugni's features homemade chili, minestrone soup, and the house specialty—sandwiches so large they border on the ridiculous ($2.44). In addition, the deli counter displays a variety of goodies including salads, hot chili, pasta and soup. Between the infectious humor of proprietors and the quality of the food, customers usually exit smiling.

W.F. Giugni & Son Grocery Co., 1227 Main St. St. Helena 94574. Telephone (707) 963-3421. Hours: 8:00 a.m. - 6:00 p.m., daily. No Cards.

ST. HELENA DELI AND FINE FOODS — *Provisions, Deli*

Fresh brewed coffee, croissants, pasta salad, stuffed grape leaves and homemade soups are just a few of the items available at the St. Helena Deli and Fine Foods, located just off highway 29. Owners Lynn and Rosilyn Parkering take pride in offering a multitude of hot and cold sandwiches, cheeses, and various imported treats from around the world.

Their Wine Room offers a fine selection of California Wines. You may also select a favorite kitchen gadget, poster or book.

Italian food enthusiasts will enjoy the assorted pastas offered in the dining room. Outdoor seating available. Picnic lunches to go.

St. Helena Deli and Fine Foods, 61 Main St., St. Helena 94574. Telephone (707) 963-3235. Hours: 9:00 a.m. - 6:30 p.m. daily. Price range: $1.00 - $4.50. Seating 75.

LA BELLE HELENE   *Restaurant*

La Belle Helene is a provincial French restaurant located in a Nineteenth Century stone edifice on a quiet side street. Snowy-white tablecloths and Oriental rugs and tapestries help create an ambiance of informal elegance.

This restaurant, at its best, offers one of the finest dining experiences in the Napa Valley. The highly individualized approach and an ever-changing menu offer the possibility of supreme success with only an occasional disappointment.

Menu choices, presented to the table on a chalkboard, might range from veal sauteed with shallots and mushrooms to filet of sole poached in wines with a cream and mushroom sauce. Entrees are served with vegetable garnish and a superb cream soup. The highly recommended luncheon might well feature the delightful Salad Nicoise or any number of dinner entrees at lower than dinner prices. Special care is taken with the meticulously presented homemade tortes and French pastries.

Lunches at La Belle Helene are unhurried, uncrowded, and unreservedly recommended. The wine list offers carefully selected wines from Napa Valley's finest vineyards. A new cafe has opened, featuring a mequite grill, where lunch and a la carte dinner is served.

La Belle Helene, 1345 Railroad Ave., St. Helena 94574. Telephone (707) 963-1234. Hours: Lunch 11:30 a.m. - 4:00 p.m. Dinner 5:30 p.m. - 9:00 p.m. Price range: Lunch, $7.00 - $11.00, Dinner $13.95 - $20.00. Corkage $3.00 Reservations suggested.

Travel Notes: _____

_____

_____

FREEMARK ABBEY   *Restuarant, Provisions*

The Freemark Abbey complex is the busiest tourist stop in Napa Valley. The old stone winery houses Hurds Gifts & Gourmet, Hurd Beeswax Candle Factory and the Abbey Restaurant. The gourmet shop is noted for their encyclopedic offering of kitchen utensils as well as imported and domestic honeys, jams, cookies, breads, cheeses, and teas. Also proffered are unusual wine accessories and a comprehensive selection of wine and cooking books.

Hurds Gifts and Gourmet, 3020 St. Helena Hwy., St. Helena 94574. Telephone (707) 963-3303. Hours: Summer, 9:30 a.m. - 6:00 p.m. daily; Winter, weekdays 9:30 a.m. - 5:30 p.m., weekend 10:00 a.m. - 5:30 p.m. Cards: BA, MC.

PALMER'S ESPRESSO BAR AND CAFE   *Cafe*

St. Helena is inexorably metamorphosing from a sleepy village into a Napa Valley cultural center. The people here take wine and food seriously. On occasion their avocation gets out of hand and turns into a profession. Such is the case with the owners of Palmers. They have opened a very civilized little cafe in downtown St. Helena. It is open six days a week from 7:30 a.m. until midnight; always available are fresh croissants, espresso, bagels and creme fraiche for breakfast, daily specials, and platters of cheese and meats. A different salad is prepared daily. Specially selected wines are available by the taste and the glass. On Sundays they serve a brunch that is the talk of the town.

Palmer's Espresso Bar and Cafe, 1313 Main Street, St. Helena 94574. Telephone (707) 963-1788. Hours: 8:00 a.m. - 10:00 p.m., Tues. - Sun. Price range: breakfast $2.00 - $7.00; lunch and dinner $3.50 - $7.00. Open for Sunday Brunch. No cards accepted.Seating: 50.

MEADOWOOD   *A Private Reserve*

This private club is nestled in a secluded canyon outside of St. Helena. The road winds along a shady creekbed, strewn with moss-covered boulders and ferns, and ends at the comfortable clubhouse where guests dine high above the idyllic nine-hole golf course and sip wine by member vintners.

Under the culinary guidance of Chef Hale Lake, Meadowood offers one of California's finest dining experiences. Lake is a master in the subtle artistry of presentation, reflecting nuances from both Japanese and Novelle Cuisine.

The whims of the chef and availability of fresh ingredients demand a constantly changing menu — a menu so innovative that it can prove downright dangerous to the true gourmand. Each dish is so tempting it is almost impossible not to over indulge. A hypothetical four course meal might include an appetizer of paper thin onion rings, fettucini with pancetta, pesto and cream sauce, perfectly grilled Alaskan Salmon with saffron and citron sauce, followed by espresso and delicate chocolate crepes covered with fresh fruit and creme fraiche. (see sample menu page 44).

Meadowood is at the very heart of the Napa Valley Wine Community. The Vintner's Association maintains a permanent office here and the gala annual Wine Auction in June has become the most prestigious social event of the year attracting 2,500 wine enthusiasts from around the world.

The club already includes a 9-hole golf course, tennis courts, pool and guest lodging. Soon to be added are spa and health facilities, a conference center and a limited number of private cluster lodges tucked away in the hills.

Meadowood, 900 Meadowood Lane, St. Helena 94574. Telephone (707) 963-3646.
Hours: Dinner Wed. - Sun. 6:00 - 9:00. Price range: $18.80 - $22.80. Cards: VISA, MC, AMEX.
Reservations required. Seating: 60.
Lodging: Call Meadowood for further information.

MIRAMONTE RESTAURANT & INN

Restaurant, Inn

The stark decor is reminiscent of a baronial hunting lodge. A large fireplace dominates one wall, deer antler chandelliers provide the dim lighting. A somewhat incongruous setting for what is undoubtably Napa Valley's best restaurant.

The co-owners of the Miramonte have impeccable credentials in the world of cuisine. Swiss born Eduoard Platel, a precise restaurant management specialist, was Director of the California Culinary Institute when he met partner Udo Nechutnys. Udo began his apprenticeship as a French chef at 17, and in the course of his career has been at Maxim's in Paris and spent four years working with Paul Bocuse of nouvelle cuisine fame.

The ever-changing menu is offered on either a prix fixe or a la carte basis. The food is invariably fresh, expertly prepared and is a pleasure to the eye as well as the palate. As an example, the aignilettes canard with sauce poiveres vert - medallions of rare duck breast with a green peppercorn sauce is a unique and sumptuous dish. It might come artfully served with buttery rounds of zucchini, golden crusty pomme de terre anna, shitaki mushrooms sauteed in wine, butter, and cream. The wine list is well selected and priced reasonably.

Miramonte Restaurant & Country Inn. 1327 Railroad Ave., St. Helena 94574. Telephone (707) 963-3970. Hours: Dinner at 6:15 - 9:00 p.m. daily except Monday and Tuesday. Price range: $24.00 - $27.00. Corkage: $5.00. Two rooms are available at $55.00 and $65.00. No credit cards accepted. Reservations advised.

*Travel Notes:*_____
_____
_____
_____

KAREN MITCHELL & CO.
Provisions, Catering

This small "Charcuterie" styled kitchen is located in an alleyway behind Main Street - the best kept secret in St. Helena.

Local chef Karen Mitchell, prepares all her food from fresh ingredients on the premises.

The selection varies with the season and whims of the chef. Typical take-out and picnic fare includes: local cheeses, pates, galatines, a large salad selection, baguettes, and assorted desserts. Umbrella tables are available for lunching on the spot. Box lunches can be ordered for large groups.

Special-order cooking and catering are the mainstay of the business. Parties are catered locally for as few as 8 or as many as 500. Summer feasts often feature Karen's large portable barbecues grilling fresh spring lamb, local seafood or a side of beef.

Karen Mitchell & Co., 1341 Money Way, (in the alley west of Main St.,) St. Helena 94574. Telephone (707) 963-9731. Hours: 10:00 a.m. - 6:00 p.m. Tues. - Sat.

ROSE et LE FAVOUR
Restaurant

Napa Valley now has more French restaurants per capita than anywhere outside of France, but then Napa Valley is more like France than any place in America. The fact that the Valley can support all these restaurants is a function of the fact that each offers a unique variation on the common theme.

Cee Rose and Bruce LeFavour envisioned the perfect restaurant, one based on their years in the business and their individual ideas of perfection. That they have accomplished this is a heartwarming tale of a dream come true.

Rose et LeFavour is a tiny little island of luxuriousness located somewhat incongrously on Main Street in St. Helena. The atmosphere is one of restrained decadence — starched white table cloths festooned with exotic floral arrangements, expensive china and diners speaking in whispers.

Ever a charming hostess, Cee presides over the dining room while Bruce works his alchemy in the kitchen, creating a surprising and eclectic combination of dishes for the evening's dining experience (see sample menu page 45). You be assured you will be in for some surprises, not the least of which is the bill. Be prepared for a night of utter indulgence.

The real highlight of this establishment is the spectacular wine list. Rose et Le Favour has, beyond a doubt, the most comprehensive wine list in the Valley. Its breadth and depth is guaranteed to bring tears to the eyes of any true wine enthusiast. If you have never had the experience of drinking a twenty year old First Growth or Grand Cru, you really have not lived.

Rose et LeFavour, 1420 Main St., St. Helena 94574. Telephone (707) 963-1681. Hours: Wed. - Sat. 6:30 - 8:30 p.m. Sun. 1 - 3 p.m., 6:30 - 8:30 p.m. Price: $45.00. Seating: 30. No cards. Reservations advised.

ST. GEORGE
Restaurant, Bar

Walking up the steps to the massive doorway of St. George, one cannot but be vaguely reminded of the pyramid builder's monuments. Owner Newton Cope refers to it as "a poor man's Hearst Castle." Inside, thirty foot high walls display colossal nudes resplendent in framed Rococo gold leaf.

At night St. George serves Italian food, but at lunch, beautifully presented fresh salads, sandwiches and the enormous lamburghini (lamb burger) augment the menu. During the summer lunches are served outside in a quiet walled patio. The bar is justifiably very popular with the locals.

St. George, 1050 Charter Oak Ave., St. Helena 94574. Telephone (707) 963-7938. Hours: Daily, Lunch 11:30 a.m. - 2:30 p.m.; Dinner, 5:30 - 9:30 p.m. Price range: Lunch $4.00 - $8.00, Dinner $9.00 - $17.00. Corkage: $4.00. Full bar service. Reservations suggested. Cards: AE, VISA, MC. Seating: 120-180.

SPRING STREET   *Restaurant*

Fairly new on the block, the Spring Street Restaurant has been pleasantly remodeled, very airy, with seating on multileveled patios and decks. The luncheon menu is simple, but quite good. The moderately priced menu features several fresh and interesting salads, quiches, homemade soups and desserts.

Spring Street, 1245 Spring St., St. Helena 94574. Telephone (707) 963-5578. Hours: Lunch 11:00 a.m. - 2:30 p.m. weekdays. Price range: $2.00 - $7.00. Cards: VISA, MC. Seating capacity 60 including patio.

V. SATTUI WINERY   *Provisions*

Provisions offered for sale include ten dozen cheeses, salami, homemade pate and cheesecake, local walnuts, apples, fruit and fresh French bread. A home-smoked cheddar cheese and homemade chocolate truffles are also to be found here.

Redwood counters atop old barrels display wine books, crystal glassware, baskets, and gourmet accessories. Patrons are encouraged to picnic among the walnut trees.

V. Sattui Winery, White Lane, St. Helena 94574. Telephone (707) 963-7774. Hours: Summer, 9:00 a.m. - 6:00 p.m.; Winter 9:00 a.m. - 5:30 p.m. Cards: BA, MC. Seating capacity 18 picnic tables.

Travel Notes: _____

_____

_____

ST. HELENA

CALISTOGA

NAPA VALLEY OLIVE OIL MFG. CO. *Provisions*

Upon entering the "Olive Oil Factory", owners Osvaldo Particelli and Policarpo Lucchesi are likely to be engaged in lively debate, but unless the visitor speaks Italian, he won't know whether the topic is the price of olives or Roman politics. Olive oil is still produced here as it has been for nearly a century, but the emphasis is on cheese, salami, and Italian foods. Two counters are packed with quality cheeses of every size and shape, all at surprisingly low prices.

Napa Valley Olive Oil Manufacturing Co., 835 McCorkle Ave., St. Helena 94574. Telephone (707) 963-4173. Hours: 8 a.m. - 5:30 p.m., daily except holidays. No cards. Seating capacity: two picnic tables.

CEMENT WORKS *Grocery, Restaurant, Bar, Shops*

The old Cement Works had been abandoned for many years when Jim Hayhoe began his extensive redevelopment project. Just completed, the handsome new complex houses ten shops, a restaurant, a pub and a bar, along with a scenic three acrea picnic area.

The Wineworks is a retail gem. A spectacular produce section features exotica such as fresh water chestnuts, shitaki, enoki mushrooms, endive, cherimoya and local chantrelles. The packaged foods section is a gourmet's delight which puts Oakville Grocery to shame. In the deli section, fresh sausages, cold salads, and a dizzying array of cheeses are featured. Local wines are available for tasting.

The Best Cellar is an ecclectic blend of bookstore, espresso bar, restaurant and cocktail lounge. Fresh croissants are available for light breakfasts, lunches boast one of the Valley's best cheeseburgers. Pasta is the mainstay of the moderately priced dinners.

The Fox and Hounds is a real novelty in the Wine Country. It is an authentic reproduction of a traditional English Pub. Both beer and champagne are on tap to accompany fish and chips, bangers and mash.

La Dolce Prima is an exquisite little ice creamery specializing in exotic Italian delights. Perfect for those sweltering Napa Valley summers.

The Cement Works, 3111 N. St. Helena Hwy., St. Helena 94574, telephone: (707) 963-1261. Wine Works, Telephone (707) 963-9484 — hours: 10:00 - 6:00. The Best Cellar (707) 963-5217. The Fox and Hounds — hours: 11 - 11 daily.

Travel Notes; _____

_____

_____

33

CALISTOGA INN   *Restaurant, Inn*

The Calistoga Inn succeeds admirably in being everything that the word "Inn" implies. Here the weary traveller can find generous and impeccably prepared meals, nightly accommodations and a convivial evening gathering place.

The heart of this cozy establishment is the kitchen where husband and wife chefs Audrey Holman and Frank Doffey preside over simmering pots of rich stocks for soups and sauces. The ever-changing menu is created around seasonally available produce, a third of which is comprised of the housespeciality — seafood, always absolutely fresh and prepared with style and skill. One might find poached salmon with cucumber Hollandise or Petrale Sole Meuniere lightly grilled in butter. The wine list is excellent and reasonably priced.

Proprietor Phil Rogers sets the relaxed and friendly tone and assures that every visit is a pleasure. Other attractions are the outdoor patio, for special events and the well stocked bar which, in the evenings, is patronized by a gregarious cross section of locals.

Calistoga Inn, 1250 Lincoln Ave., Calistoga 94515. Telephone (707) 942-4101. Hours: Weekdays, 5:30 - 9:30 p.m., weekends, 5:00 - 10:00 p.m., closed Monday. Price range: Dinner, from $10.15 - $12.50. Corkage $3.00. Cards: VISA, MC. Full bar. Reservations recommended.

SILVERADO RESTAURANT   *Restaurant, Tavern*

The effusive country hospitality of the Napa Valley is nowhere more evident than here. Host and sommellier Alix Dierkhising is one of the most knowledgeable wine enthusiasts in the Valley and can usually be enticed into a lively enological discussion. The impressive wine list features over 200 personally selected bottles, most of which are also available for off sale. This is a family operation, with brother Mark presiding over the kitchen.

The Tavern is one of the better in the upper Valley; a number of interesting wines are always available by the glass or taste. The back bar is a Baroque specimen brought around Cape Horn in 1895. Formal wine tastings are scheduled almost weekly, and are well attended by local vintners and winery workers.

Dinner menu selections emphasize freshness and simplicity, and the owners term the cuisine style "New American." Several nightly specials, usually including seasonal fish, augment the standard entree items of beef, veal, lamb, chicken and seafood, these often served with light sauces. A great favorite with Valley residents is the Hanging Beef buffet held every Wednesday night. Desserts are also kept "in the family" with Mark's wife Dawn creating fresh-daily pastries.

Silverado Restaurant and Tavern, 1374 Lincoln Ave., Calistoga 94515. Telephone (707) 942-6725. Hours: 7:00 a.m. - 10:00 p.m. daily. Price range: Breakfast, $2.50 - $5.00; Lunch, $3.00 - $7.50; Dinner, $5.50 - $13.00. Corkage $5.00. Full bar. No cards. Reservations suggested. Catering available. Seating 136.

Travel Notes: _____

_____

_____

Menus

The editors have had numerous requests to provide a qualitative listing of Napa Valley restaurants. While it should be remembered that restaurants selected for review in the Napa Valley Wine Tour appear here only because they are in some way noteworthy, we have decided to further qualify restaurants by selecting—through a polling system—the "Ten Best Napa Valley Restaurants". These have been selected by a representative group of Napa Valley Vintners as being their "favorite" restaurants.

We have tried to provide not only a broad geographical distribution but have singled out which meals are the most favored in each particular restaurant. The top ten restaurants are represented in this section by reproductions of their menus.

PLEASE NOTE:

Menus and prices will change. Some restaurants included in this section have a policy of changing their menus daily or weekly. These menus are included only to give an indication of menu and price range. One further note: we have found it impossible to limit the number of restaurants to 10; the careful reader will find that we have actually included eleven.

DOMAINE CHANDON
California Drive, Yountville, CA 94599 (707) 944-2467
''Lunch'' or ''Dinner''

LA SOUPE DE SAISON
Soup of the season — 3.80

CREME DE TOMATES EN CROUTE
Tomato soup in puff pastry — 4.20

Les Entrées Froides

SALADE D'ENDIVE ET CRESSON
Belgium endive and water cress salad — 4.20

TERRINE DE CANARD AU COGNAC
Duck terrine with cognac — 5.80

LES ASPERGES MOUSSELINE
Asparagus with mousseline sauce — 5.20

LA GALANTINE DE COQUILLES
ST. JACQUES ET SAUMON
Scallops and salmon terrine — 4.80

Les Entrées Chaudes

LE BOUQUETS ROSES AU FENOUIL
Fresh prawns with fennel and beurre blanc — 6.80

L'OEUF MOSCOVITE
Poached egg with smoked salmon,
caviar and Hollandaise sauce — 5.20

PATES FRAICHES AU SAFRAN AVEC LES MOULES
Fresh saffron pasta with mussels — 5.20

Les Poissons

LE BAR EN CROUTE, SAUCE CHORON
Sea bass in puff pastry with choron sauce — 8.80

LE SAUMON AUX POIVRONS
Salmon with red and green bell pepper sauce — 9.80

LA LOTTE AU THYM ET LAURIER
SUR EPINARDS
Angler fish with champagne sauce on spinach — 9.80

Les Viandes et Volailles

LE JAMBONNEAU DE CANARD AUX RAISINS
Stuffed duck legs with raisin sauce — 8.20

LE RIS DE VEAU A L'OSEILLE ET JUS DE TRUFFLE
Sweetbreads with sorrel and truffle juice — 9.80

L'AGNEAU AU ROMARIN ET VINAIGRE BALSAMIQUE
Lamb with rosemary and balsamic vinegar sauce — 8.80

L'ENTRECOTE A L'ECHALOTTE
New York strip with shallot sauce — 9.20

THE DINER

6476 Washington St., Yountville, CA 94599 (707) 944-2626

''Breakfast'' or ''Lunch''

BREAKFAST

Served all day.

OMELETTES

Our three-egg omelette comes with home-style grilled potatoes or fruit cup and your choice of toasts.

1. MUSHROOM and onion 4.21
   with swiss cheese, add 75
   with sour cream, add 50
2. CHEESE cheddar, monterey jack
   or swiss 4.25
   with ham, add 75
3. AVOCADO & SOUR CREAM . . 4.25
   with bacon bits, add 75
4. MEXICAN fresh tomatoes, jack
   cheese, olives, homemade
   chile sauce 4.25
5. GREEN CHILE & CHEESE 4.25
   cheddar or jack
6. YOUR SPECIAL create your own:
   start with a plain omelette 3.50
   add .52   for each:
   mushrooms, tomatoes, onions,
   green chiles, sour cream, or chile sauce
   add .75   for each:
   avocado, ham, bacon bits, or cheese

The All-American

Two eggs, home-style grilled potatoes or fruit cup, toast, and choice of meat:

   Ham, sausage, smokey links,
   bacon or beef patty.   4.25
   Without meat   2.75

Seasoned Potatoes

Home-style grilled potatoes, with onions, herbs, and cheddar cheese.

   side order 152
   w/egg dishes . . .1.00

Breads

Your choice of sliced french bread, russian rye, or wheatberry.
English muffin
   add: .15

HOUSE SPECIALTIES

1. HUEVOS RANCHEROS A concoction of basted eggs, jack and cheddar cheeses,
sour cream, homemade chile sauce and corn tortillas, w/grilled potatoes 5.25
2. THE SANTA MONICA SPECIAL A large grilled omelette with tortilla strips,
green onions, jack cheese and salsa. Comes with grilled potatoes and toast. 4.95
3. SCRAMBLED HAM AND EGGS Thin strips of sauteed ham cooked with scrambled eggs.
Comes with grilled potatoes and toast. 4.25
4. CRISPY CORNMEAL PANCAKES Four southern-style corn cakes, served with
smokey links and basted eggs. Try them with boysenberry syrup 5.25
5. FRENCH TOAST Your choice of french or wheatberry bread, dipped in eggs,
and grilled, served with whipped butter and syrup or brown sugar 2.95
6. GERMAN POTATO PANCAKES Shredded potatoes in a light egg batter with
herbs, served with sausage and applesauce 5.25
7. COUNTRY BREAKFAST Two fluffy buttermilk pancakes, sausage and one
basted egg 4.95
8. OLD FASHIONED OATMEAL Made to order with raisins, nuts, butter, brown
sugar, and milk on the side 1.95
9. BUTTERMILK PANCAKES Fluffy Large pancakes. Short stack (2) 3.20
   Tall stack (4) 4.00
10. JACK'S SPECIAL Grilled french bread, topped with sausage patty and
one basted egg. With potatoes or fruit cup. 3.95
11. FRESH FRUIT AND YOGURT A bowl of fresh seasonal fruits, topped with
our mild homemade yogurt 3.25

Side Orders

Smokey links or ham 1.95
Bacon, sausage or beef patty 1.75
Yogurt 1.00
Fresh fruit cup 1.50
Fruit in season 75-1.25
Eggs, each 75
Grilled potatoes 85
Toast 52
English muffin 65

Beverages

Coffee 52
Tea: *eng breakfast* 60
   Herbal 60
Juice: tomato, orange,
   apple or apricot 60-.85
Milk: 60-.85
Fresh squeezed juice (when available) . . .1.50
Hot chocolate made with
real milk and chocolate
topped with whipped cream 95

37

THE FRENCH LAUNDRY MENU

JANUARY 12, 1983

APPETIZERS

ARTICHOKE WITH GARLIC MAYONNAISE
SAUTÉED SCALLOPS WITH BACON AND VERMOUTH
SMOKED TROUT

TONIGHT'S DINNER

TORTILLA SOUP

SUPREMES OF CHICKEN WITH LEMON AND MINT CREAM

SALAD OF BUTTER LETTUCE AND SPINACH
WITH CHEESES

DESSERTS COFFEE

BLUEBERRY CREAM CHEESE TORTE
APRICOT CHOCOLATE MERINGUES
ORANGES ORIENTALE

PRICE $30.00   SERVICE 15%

Appetizers, Soups and Salads

Homemade Soup Daily..	$2.00
Grilled Duck Liver, Chicken Filet and smoked Bacon Skewer....	4.25
Smoked Tenderloin, virgin olive oil, parmesan, fresh herbs...	3.50
Cornmeal Pancake with homemade sour cream and Caviar........	4.80
Warm Goat Cheese, almond coated with herb vinaigrette.......	3.95
Chinese Chicken Salad......................................	6.95
Mixed Greens, Bleu Cheese, smoked Bacon and seasoned Walnuts.	3.50

From the Wood Burning Oven

Half slab Barbequed Baby Back Ribs........................	8.65
Smoked Lemon Chicken and Polenta..........................	7.85
Smoked Pork Loin with Apple Lemon sauce and black beans......	7.90
Lightly smoked then pan fried Prawns......................	9.95

From the Mesquite Grill

Fresh Fish (see chalkboard)	
Pounded Chicken Breast with Avocado salsa....................	7.85
Calf's Liver with Tomatoes, grilled Onions and Bacon........	8.50
Sonoma Rabbit with green Onion and mustard vinaigrette......	8.95
Skirt Steak, marinated in soy and ginger...................	6.90
Veal Loin with rosemary butter.............................	9.85

Sandwiches

Hamburger or Cheeseburger...................................	4.95
Smoked Turkey Breast, Avocado and Bacon....................	5.80
Filet Mignon, grilled Onions and Watercress.................	6.95

Sides and Condiments

Onion Rings..	1.95
Grilled Eggplant and Onions with ginger butter..............	3.40
Oven Roasted New Potatoes...................................	2.25
Roasted Garlic...	1.00
Tomato Chutney...	.95
Polenta..	.95
Black Beans & Rice, chopped red onions, cilantro, sour cream.	2.10

Desserts

Chocolate Pecan Cake, chocolate sauce......................	3.25
Ice Cream..	2.50
Apple Dumpling, bourbon cream..............................	3.45
Tapioca Pudding..	2.20

Hors d'Oeuvres

Cornet d'œufs de caille, aux petits légumes verts
PASTRY CONE WITH POACHED QUAIL EGGS AND FRESH VEGETABLES

Pâtes fraîches aux truffes
FRESH LINGUINI WITH TRUFFLE SAUCE

Boudin de fruits de mer au beurre blanc
HOT SEAFOOD SAUSAGE

Huîtres pochées au vermouth
FRESH OYSTERS POACHED IN VERMOUTH

Feuilleté d'escargots, à la pointe d'ail
SNAILS IN PASTRY SHELL, GARLIC CREAM SAUCE

Le potage du chef

Entrées

Homard du Maine selon ma façon (en saison)
CHEF'S MAINE LOBSTER ($5.50 extra)

Truite saumonée, au beurre d'oursins
POACHED SALMON TROUT, SEA URCHIN BUTTER SAUCE

Suprême de canard au poivre rose
FILET OF DUCKLING WITH PINK PEPPERCORN

Petites cailles de la vallée
ROASTED FARM QUAILS, GAME SAUCE

Sauté de ris de veau aux écrevisses
SAUTÉ OF SWEETBREADS WITH CRAYFISH

Escalopes de veau forestière, foie blond
VEAL SCALLOPS WITH MUSHROOMS, BLONDE LIVER MOUSSE

Côtes d'agneau, vert pré
BROILED LAMB CHOPS, GARDEN VEGETABLES

Entrecôte de bœuf grillée, beurre rouge
BROILED SIRLOIN, BORDELAISE BUTTER

Mignon de bœuf aux perles noires
FILET OF BEEF WITH TRUFFLE SAUCE AND PISTACHIOS

Salade verte et fromage de chèvre

Friandises

Soufflé du jour ($2.00 extra)

Mousse au chocolat noir
BLACK CHOCOLATE MOUSSE

Assiette du gourmand ($2.00 extra)
SWEET PLATE

Soufflé glacé de la maison
ICED SOUFFLÉ

Sorbets de fruits de saison
ASSORTMENT OF FRESH FRUIT SHERBETS

Thé, Café, Décaf

$34.00

Infusion d'herbes, espresso, décaf espresso $2.00

St. George

ENTREES
GARNISHED WITH VEGETABLES

CHEFS SPECIAL ....

PASTA OF THE DAY 6.95

LINGUINE WITH CLAM SAUCE 5.50

LASAGNE PASTICCIATE 5.75
Baked Lasagne with meat sauce.

POLLO E PROSCIUTTO 6.00
Sliced cold breast of chicken with
prosciutto and fresh herb mayonnaise.

CHIPPOLATA SAUTE 5.75
Sausage with bell peppers, onions, and mushrooms.

STUFFED CHICKEN BREAST 6.50
Stuffing varies daily.

SAUTEED SOLE 7.50
When available.

SOUP AND SALAD 5.00

SALADS
CHOICE OF OIL AND VINEGAR, BLUE CHEESE, OR CREAMY TARRAGON

SPECIAL SALAD 5.95

INSALATA MISTA 2.50
Small tossed green salad.

MEDITERRANEAN SALAD 5.25

CRAB AND SHRIMP SALAD 6.25

MIRAMONTE RESTAURANT & INN

1327 Railroad Ave., St. Helena, CA 94574 (707) 963-3970

''Dinner''

Mousseline d'Epinard

Filet de Sole ''Albert''

Poularde a la creme aux
Champignons de Chine

Salade verte

Dessert Miramonte

$30.00

A la Carte . . .

Sabayon de Tortue
ou
Jambon de Westphalie

Saumon fume
ou
Gateau de Foie de Volaille
Paul Bocuse

Piece de Boeuf a la Moelle
Sauce Bourguignonne
ou
Aignilette de Canard
sauce poivre verts

Salade verte

Dessert Miramonte

$27.00

Pate de saumon ''Pyramide''

La Terrine de Canard ''Bocuse''

La salade de Canard Fume

Asparagus Mousseline

All food produce is fresh and selected for its prime quality within its season and market availability. Our menu is planned in conformity with this precept. we prefer to be out of a particular dish temporarily rather than to compromise the fine quality of our food.

—LA—BELLE—HELENE—RESTAURANT—
1345 Railroad Avenue   St. Helena, CA 94574   707-963-1234

Philippe Bonnafont de Tauzia, host

AUTUMN / WINTER 1982
Sample Menus

LUNCH 11:30 am - 3:00 pm
à la carte
ranges from $6.00 to $10.00

DINNER 5:30 - 10:00 pm
served with soup and salad
ranges from $14.50 to $20.00

---
hors d'oeuvres
---

mousse de foie de canard
(duck liver mousse)

pâté brioché
(pâté in brioche dough)

---
soups
---

crème de laitue
(cream of lettuce soup)

crème du Barry
(cream of cauliflower)

---
entrees
---

truite au champagne
(trout poached in champagne)

crêpes au jambon
(crêpes w / ham & cheese sauce)

pot au feu
(boiled brisket of beef w / vegetables)

lapin forestière
(rabbit braised w / red wine)

poulet à l'ail
(sautéed chicken w / garlic sauce)

poulet grand mère Bise
(marinated chicken breast)

espadon grillé au Pernod
(grilled Sword fish w / Pernod)

gigot d'agneau rôti aux herbes
(roasted leg of lamb w / herbs)

sauté de veau aux épinards
(sautéed veal w / spinach sauce)

faisan vallée d'Auge
(roasted pheasant w / apples & brandy)

oie braisée aux marrons
(braised goose w / chestnut stuffing)

filet de boeuf aux chanterelles
(grilled filet of beef w / red wine)

---
fromages

(assorted cheeses)

---
desserts
---

crème caramel, mousse au chocolat, chocolate cheesecake, tarte aux fraises,
tarte aux noix, sorbet aux ananas

and the best of Napa Valley wines

Open Wednesday through Monday (closed Tuesday)
We will be closed Thanksgiving Day. The restaurant will be open in December.
except for Christmas Eve and Christmas Day.
Make your New Year's Eve reservations now!

900 MEADOWOOD LANE ST. HELENA, CALIFORNIA 94574 (707) 963-3646

BUNDENFLEISCH WITH CORNICIONS AND NICOISE OLIVES

BROILED BLUE POINT OYSTERS WITH A DILL GLACAGE 1.75 extra

VEAL AND VENISON PATE WITH TOMATO CHUTNEY AND CHINESE MUSTARD SAUCE

SMOKED STURGEON AND GRAVALOX WITH CAPERS, SHALLOTS AND BERMUDA ONIONS

*

POTATO AND LEEK POTAGE

*

FRESH HAWAIIAN YELLOWFIN TUNA WITH SAUCE HUNAN

GRILLED COLUMBIA RIVER STURGEON WITH TOASTED HAZELNUTS AND SAUCE FLORENTINE

NORTH EASTERN YELLOWTAIL SOLE WITH FRESH ASPARAGUS, GLACE DE POISSON AND
LOBSTER GARNI 2.00 extra

FRESH ATLANTIC TILE FISH WITH SAUCE GRENOBLE

SAUTEED SCALLOPS WITH PAPAYA AND TOASTED PINE NUTS

GRILLED FILET OF FRESH ALASKAN SALMON WITH SAUCE CITRON

BREAST OF LONG ISLAND DUCK WITH PORT WINE SAUCE AND COMICE PEARS

RACK OF LAMB WITH PERSIALLADE AND MADEIRA SAUCE

MILK-FED VEAL PAILLARDS WITH TOMATO AND GARLIC BUTTER

NEW YORK STEAK WITH OYSTER MUSHROOMS AND SAUCE BORDELAISE

LOIN OF CANADIAN ELK WITH SAUCE ROBERT 15.00 extra

MEADOWOOD MEMBERS SPECIAL

*

MEADOWOOD SALAD

BELGIAN ENDIVE SALAD WITH BACON AND HAZELNUT VINAIGRETTE .75 extra

*

FRESH FRUIT TART

CHOCOLATE BOMBE CAKE

NEW YORK STYLE CHEESECAKE

CHOCOLATE CREPES WITH WHITE CHOCOLATE MOUSSE AND FRESH FRUIT

LEMON SOUFFLE WITH FRESH STRAWBERRY SAUCE 1.75 extra

FRESH FRUIT AND CHEESES .75 extra

Three Courses $18.80   Four Courses $22.80

Rose et he Favour

March 17, 1983

A Bit of the Bubbly

Salmon Caviar with Champagne/Sour Cream
Foie Blond with Champagne Vinegar
Belon Oysters with Champagne Sauce

Yellowfin Tuna, Grilled Rare
Herb Butter and Eggplant

Poussin and Squab with Mustard

Cheese Tray

Dessert Cart

$40.00

March 23

Appetizers:
  Duck liver mousse 2.75
  Oregon blue cheese mousse 2.75
  Ceviche of bay scallops, Loreto 4.25
  Steamed softshell clams, garlic & vermouth 5.50

Soup and salad (à la carte):
  Cream of spinach soup 2.50
  Tossed green salad, house dressing 2.50

Entrees - served with soup or salad:
  Petrale sole meunière 10.50
  Grilled Pacific grouper, mushroom sauce 12.50
  Grilled halibut, pecan brown butter 12.50
  Grilled swordfish, caper sauce 12.50
  Sauteed Florida sea scallops, garlic sauce 12.50
  Fish stew, Calistoga Inn 10.50
  Braised duck, cassis sauce 13.50
  Braised veal, tarragon & mushroom sauce 12.50
  Broiled rib-eye steak, herb butter 14.50
  Fettuccine verde with smoked mussels & saffron sauce 12.50

Desserts:
  Creme caramel 2.50
  Italian cream with raspberry sauce 2.50
  Chocolate cake with strawberries & creme fraiche 3.00
  Poached pear, creme Anglaise, chocolate sauce 3.00

Lodging

isitors have been travelling Napa's "Wine Road" for over a century enjoying the conviviality and famous hospitality of the region. Robert Louis Stevenson honeymooned here in 1880 and tells the engaging story of his visit in *Silverado Squatters,* penning these inspired words: "The stirring sunlight and the growing vines and the vats and bottles in the cavern made a pleasant music for the mind. Here also the earth's cream was being skimmed and garnered. . .and the wine is bottled poetry."

There is something very special about drinking wine where it is made. After all, wine is a reflection of a mingling of sun, soil and man. Sipping wine while surrounded by the barrels, crushers and presses, inhaling the winery breath that steals from the walls and ceilings, inextricably binds one to the moment. A visitor may find need of a place to rest, to sort out the tastes and sights he has experienced.

The following information has been provided to aid the overnight guest. The hotels, inns, resorts, spas and campground reviewed offer a variety of lodgings, many amid rural vineyard settings and in keeping with the Napa Valley's time honored tradition of gracious hospitality.

Accommodations in Napa Valley are somewhat limited; therefore, reservations are suggested to insure against disappointment. For visits during the busiest touring months from May to November, reservations thirty to sixty days in advance are advised. For those travelling during winter months, a day's notice should be sufficient.

PLEASE NOTE: There are quite a few small bed and breakfast inns in the valley, more than can be enumerated in this volume. If you can't find accommodations, the people at the Bed and Breakfast Exchange can help; call 963-7756.

THE CHATEAU   *Hotel*

Napa has a new luxury hotel, unlike its competition to the south, Chateau has a somewhat more wine-oriented program.

The entire structure was designed to emulate the warmth, comfort and style of a French Chateau. Complimentary wine tastings are held in the hospitality room. European style breakfasts are served on a sunny terrace (on clear days).

For those who enjoy their creature comforts The Chateau offers a pool and spa, movie channel equipped color T.V.s and phones in the rooms. Also offered is French-maid turn-down service. There are rooms available for the handicapped as well as suites for the honey-mooners and executive businessmen.

The Chateau, 4195 Solano Ave. Napa 94558. Telephone (707) 253-9300. Rates: on season, Single $66.00, Double $76.00. Suites $95.00 - $150.00. All rates include European style breakfast for two. Number of rooms 115.

Travel Notes: _____

_____

_____

HOLIDAY INN   *Hotel*

The 200 room Holiday Inn is located just off Napa City's busiest intersection. The hotel boasts a multitude of attractions including swimming pool, lighted tennis courts, hot tub, king size beds, poolside suites, banquet facilities, full bar and restaurant. There is a free airport shuttle to Napa Airport.

Holiday Inn, 3425 Solano Ave., Napa 94558. Telephone (707) 253-7433. Reservations: (800) 238-8000. Rates: $59.50 single; $67.50 double. Cards: VISA, MC, AE, DC, CB. Number of rooms: 193. Ask for off-season rates.

WINE VALLEY LODGE   *Motel*

This new structure is very conveniently located at the south end of the city of Napa, just off Imola Ave. and with easy access to either Highway 29 or Silverado Trail. The appointments are all quite modern and the facility is spotlessly clean, quite up to the standards of those accustomed to Holiday Inns and the like. All rooms are equipped with cable color T.V., telephones and air conditioning.

Wine Valley Lodge, 200 South Coombs St., Napa 94558. Telephone (707) 224-7911. Rates: Single, $34.00. Double $41.00. Family special $45.00. Cards: VISA, MC, AEX. Reservations suggested.

Travel Notes: _____

_____

_____

SILVERADO *Resort*

After the Civil War, General John Miller acquired this 1200-acre estate in the eastern foothills of Napa Valley and in 1870 he built a great mansion. As the story goes, he incorporated the original Spanish adobe on the site into the mansion walls. The estate eventually passed from Miller's daughter through two other owners. In 1966, the Hawaii based Amfac Corporation acquired the property and created the pleasure resort of Silverado.

The apartments at Silverado are owned by individuals who allow the management to rent them out when not in use. Each luxurious unit is completely furnished and offers air-conditioning, color television, private bar, fireplace and kitchen. Apartments have either a private patio or a balcony, and are clustered in groups around the eight swimming pools.

Silverado also has four attractively appointed conference rooms available to groups of varying size.

Recreational facilities include two challenging 18-hole golf courses and 20 outdoor tennis courts (each with permement viewing stands).

For convenience guests may luncheon in the Silverado Bar and Grill where the salad bar is popular, or dine in the recently opened Vintners Court. Dining in Royal Oak Room, you overlook a panorama of trees and mountains.

Silverado, 1600 Atlas Peak Road, Napa 94558. Telephone (707) 257-0200. Room rates: $85.00 - $325.00, single or double.

Travel Notes: _____

_____

_____

BURGUNDY HOUSE   *Inn*

The Burgundy House was constructed of twenty inch thick, fieldstone walls and massive handhewn posts and timbers over a century ago. Present owners Bob and Mary Keenan bought the building in 1974 to use as an antique shop. One by one, the rooms were converted to accommodate overnight guests, the antiques becoming the furniture.

The six bedrooms and three bathrooms are colorfully furnished. Each silk-sheeted antique bed is covered with a cozy-looking quilt.

Three nearby cottages, formerly the justice building and the judges house, have been remodeled to accommodate additional guests.

Burgundy House, 6711 Washington St., Yountville 94599. Telephone (707) 944-2855. Rates: $78.00 - $110.00 double occupancy. Rates include wine and breakfast. Reservations recommended. Cards: VISA, MC, AE. Number of rooms: 6, plus 2 cottages. Call for winter rates.

BORDEAUX HOUSE   *Inn*

The modernistic brick structure was designed by Bob Kennan and is operated by the Keenan family. The interior is stylishly decorated with contemporary Italian furnishings. All rooms have fireplaces, and some rooms also sport decks and patios. The exotic bathrooms feature sunken baths with windows at eye level, allowing the bather views of the vineyards and mountains beyond. Complimentary contintntal breakfasts are served around the big fireplace in the Common Room.

Bordeaux House, 6600 Washington St., Yountville 94599. Telephone (707) 944-2855. Room Rates: $99.00 - $120.00 double occupancy, rates include wine and breakfast. Reservations recommended. Number of rooms: 6. Call for winter rates.

NAPA VALLEY LODGE   *Lodge*

This new and quite luxuriously appointed lodge is located on a scenic site right off Highway 29, overlooking vineyard and a park in the quiet, little community of Yountville. Nearby are many of Napa Valley's most popular restaurants and shops.

All the spacious rooms of this mission-style facility have private balconies and enjoy idyllic views of mountains and vines.

Guests will benefit from an attention to detail seldom seen in modern hotels. All rooms are completely soundproofed and air-conditioned; each has especially-tiled lavatories, refrigerator, cable color TV, phones, and coffee makers with free coffee. Many rooms have fireplaces and kitchenettes. There are two-room suites for families and attractively decorated conference rooms for groups.

Guests can enjoy an extra large swimming pool, or relax in a hot whirlpool spa surrounded by flowers and vineyards.

A courteous staff is ready to serve guests with restaurant reservations, valet laundry service, wine tour information, select wine book sales, bicycle rentals, and advance lodging reservations.

Napa Valley Lodge Best Western, Highway 29 at Yountville, P.O. Box L, Yountville 94599. Telephone (707) 944-2468. Rates: $78.00 - $88.00 double occupancy. Cards: VISA, MC, AE, CB, DC. Number of rooms: 55. Reservations recommended.

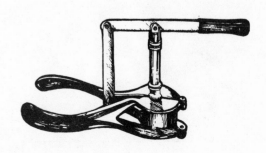

MAGNOLIA HOTEL *Inn, Restaurant*

The Magnolia Hotel traces its origin as an inn to the year 1873. In the late 1960s the entire structure was extensively renovated in keeping with the original century-old architecture. The landmark structure is owned by Bruce and Bonnie Locken and sons, Craig and Lars.

All eleven cozy guest rooms are furnished differently with antique decor, using brass beds, marble-topped washstands and dressing tables. Victorian floral-print carpet runs throughout all three floors of the venerable establishment. In addition, each room has such modern conveniences as air-conditioning and a private bath with shower.

There is even a sunken jacuzzi spa in the enclosed redwood patio, and a large swimming pool set in a garden area.

Breakfasts are served in the dining room around two large tables and might consist of orange juice or fresh fruit, hot cereal, rounds of French toast served with homemade port wine syrup, extra thick bacon and steaming hot coffee.

Magnolia Hotel, 6529 Yount St., Yountville 94599. Telephone (707) 944-2056. Room rates: double with breakfast, $75.00 - $145.00. No cards. Reservations required.

THE WEBBER PLACE *Inn*

The Webber Place is a turn-of-the-century farmhouse which has been completely renovated by schoolteacher turned carpenter and innkeeper, Loren Holte. Situated in a quiet residential neighborhood with its white picket fence and flower-bedecked front porch, the Webber Place is possessed of great natural charm.

There is plenty of privacy here; after all, only four rooms are available for rent at present. Two rooms share a bath and two have private baths. The baths are tastefully appointed in tile with brass and oak fixtures. Completely furnished with antiques and natural wood, the second story rooms overlook the surrounding houses to the mountains beyond.

The Webber Place, 6610 Webber Street, P.O. Box 2873, Yountville 94599. Telephone (707) 944-8384. Rates: $65.00 - $100.00 with continental breakfast. Cards: VISA, MC. Number of rooms: 4.

Travel Notes: _____

_____

_____

CHALET BERNENSIS   *Inn*

A native of Bern, Switzerland, pioneer John Thomann carved the name Chalet Bernensis into his stone entry gate, a name which means simply ''from Bern''. The striking gingerbread structure was originally part of the Sutter Home Winery property next door and is nearing the century mark, built in 1884. This Napa Valley landmark, now owned by Jack and Essie Doty, has four guest rooms in the main house as well as a small antique shop. These four guest rooms share two bathrooms, all on the second floor. A newly constructed tank tower patterened after the original, built nearly 100 years ago, and just adjacent to the main house, also has four guest rooms, each with private bath, gas fireplace and air conditioning.

All rooms are decorated with antiques reminiscent of an age generations removed from our own. Handmade quilts cover the twin, double or queen size beds.

The inn is conveniently located on St. Helena Highway (Hwy. 29) just south of the town limits and within walking distance of four winery tasting rooms. Picnic tables and a barbecue are available for guests to use and the wide porch is comfortably set with a swing and rocking chairs for lounging and visiting on lovely summer evenings. Tea, coffee, sherry and port are offered in the afternoon and evening. The rates include a hearty continental breakfast.

Chalet Bernensis, 225 St. Helena Hwy., St. Helena 94574. Telephone: (707) 963-4423. Rates: $54.00 and $63.00 for rooms sharing a bath; for tank tower rooms with private bath $75.00 - $99.00. Open daily. Cards: VISA, MC. Reservations suggested. Number of rooms: 9.

Travel Notes: _____

_____

_____

THE WHITE RANCH   *Inn*

The White Ranch, nestled off the beaten trail amidst a profusion of elegant, wild gardens, was built in 1865 by A. White. French doors in the single room look out on views of surrounding fields and mountains. There are miles of walking trails and guest can pick up provisions from nearby Sattui Winery for a private picnic by the river. The innkeeper Ruth Davis is a gracious country host — she even grinds her own wheat that goes into the homemade bread served with breakfast.

The White Ranch, 707 White Lane, St. Helena 94574. Telephone (707) 963-4635. Rates: $65.00. No Cards. Number of rooms: 1.

EL BONITA MOTEL   *Motel*

Hosts Rita Ryan and Jim and Susan Maloney have completed an extensive remodeling and refurnishing program at the El Bonita Motel located on Highway 29 just south of St. Helena. Care was taken to retain the motel's warmth and conviviality, yet present a bright new look.

In the courtyard surrounding the pool are sixteen rooms, each with shower, air conditioning and color television. Six garden rooms, with color T.V., are located in a wooded area at the rear of the property. These secluded units, each tastefully decorated in a different colonial style, have sliding glass doors that open into a picnic-tabled lawn. An optional kitchenette may be rented for an additional charge of $3.00 per day. Rollaway $5.00.

El Bonita Motel, 195 Main St., St. Helena 94574. Telephone (707) 963-3216. Rates: Single $32.00 - $58.00. Double $35.00 - $58.00. Cards: BA, MC. Reservations suggested. Number of rooms: 22. No pets.

HARVEST INN   *Inn*

Inkeeper Richard Geyer has indulged all his fantasies in developing the Harvest Inn. Situated in a twenty acre working vineyard on Highway 29, a new tudor-style complex is surrounded by a hand laid stone wall. Specially cast street lamps light the way to the suites, each named for a particular grape variety.

The baronial style rooms are lavishly decorated with oak antiques and queen size brass beds, tile bathrooms replete with brass and oak fixtures, pull chain toilets, and dressing vanity. Most of the rooms have fireplaces, supplied of course with firewood.

All the modern amenities are here as well. Each room is individually air conditioned, has a color television, AM-FM radio and two direct dial telephones (one in the bathroom). Most rooms have splendid views of vineyards and surrounding hillsides.

For recreation there is a swimming pool and jacuzzi, and hiking or jogging in the adjacent vineyard. Continental breakfst is served from 7:30 - 11:00 in the main lobby.

Harvest Inn, 1 Main Street, St. Helena 94574. Telephone (707) 963-WINE. Rates: $85.00 - $310.00. Cards: MC, VISA. Accommodations: 24 rooms. Reservations recommended.

THE INK HOUSE   *Inn*

This homey abode is reminiscent of the old family estate. It was built in 1884 by T.H. Ink. The sunny rooms seem virtually untouched by time since the turn of the century. An antique pump organ in the parlor is often in use in the evenings. A guest book offers comments on local restaurants and winery tasting rooms. Coffee, juice and homemade nut breads are served each morning.

The Ink House Lodgings, 1575 St. Helena Hwy., St. Helena 94574. Telephone (707) 963-3890. Rates $60.00 - $80.00. Number of rooms: 4, each with own bath. No cards, no children, smoking outside, no pets (several on premises).

CHESTELSON HOUSE   *Inn*

Claudia Chestelson is the gracious innkeeper of this elegant little establishment. The room furnishings are a tasteful combination of contemporary and Victorian. One room has its own attached bath, the other, a bath down the hall. A huge private veranda bursting with flowers surrounds the lovely Victorian house. Continental breakfast is served in the big sunny kitchen.

Chestelson House, 1417 Kearney Street, St. Helena 94574. Telephone (707) 963-2238. Rates: $75.00 - $110.00. No Cards, No pets, no children, no smoking. Number of rooms 4.

CINNAMON BEAR   *Inn*

Next door to the Chestelson House, Genny Jenkins operates this cozy bed and breakfast establishment. Genny collects bears. There are bears in the stairwell, bears in the rooms. The old fashioned rooms have high ceilings and Victorian furnishings. A large country style breakfast of eggs and spiced breads is served. The community living room offers games, color T.V. and a piano and pump organ for the guest's amusement.

Cinnamon Bear, 1407 Kearney, St. Helena 94574. Telephone (707) 963-4653. Rates: Sun. - Thurs. $68.00; Fri. & Sat. $75.00. Cards: VISA, MC. Number of rooms 4, each with private bathroom. No smoking. Pet (a cat) in residence.

HOTEL ST. HELENA   *Hotel, Wine Bar*

The Hotel St. Helena is one of Napa Valley's most historic public buildings. Much of the structures original architectual features were retained when re-modeling took place several years ago. As with the original, the Hotel's street frontage is lined with shops - some of them Napa Valley's finest, Mario's Mens Clothing and Eccola Lingerie are both outstanding.

Within the bowels of the building is secreted the Hotel St. Helena Wine Bar, an exceedingly civilized perveyor of fine wines, and attractively presented appetizers. The elegant ambiance is ideally suited for the evaluation of the great vintages of the Napa Valley, served by the glass or bottle.

The Hotel itself consists of 18 new attractive rooms, all located on the second floor of the building. The decor is a subtle blend of victorian and modern - all very artfully done with none of the kitch of Calistoga's Mount View Hotel.

The Hotel's major asset - is that it is located not only in the heart of town but also in the heart of the valley, which makes any valley excursion convenient whether it be shopping, dining or winery hopping. This major asset could pose as a drawback for some - the potentially noisy Main Street below may bother light sleepers.

Hotel St. Helena, 1309 Main St., St. Helena 94574. Telephone (707) 963-4388. Rates: $50.00 - $95.00 includes continental breakfast. Cards: VISA, MC. Reservations suggested.

Wine Bar, Telephone (707 963-9023. Hours: Price range: $1.00 - $6.75. Cards: VISA, MC.

WINE COUNTRY INN   *Inn*

Before building their country inn, Ned and Marge Smith spent a great deal of time and effort researching the traditional inns of New England. A hillside building site near Freemark Abbey was selected, not only for its exceptional view, but also its proximity to food and other provisions. Construction was totally a family effort—even Marge's octogenarian mother contributed crewel work and stitchery. Craftsmen sons Jim and Doug were responsible for the stonemasonry and woodworking. The aesthetically pleasing result is a credit to the Smith family and a tribute to the 19th Century architecture of the Napa Valley.

Each of the 25 rooms at the inn has wall-to-wall carpeting, many have fireplaces, and each is individually decorated with antique furnishings, refurbished by members of the family. Antique beds, some crowned with canopies, have been skillfully adapted to accommodate queen-size mattresses. Hand-made quilts are the perfect final touch to these unique rooms. Every room has a view; some have private balconies, and others, patios leading to the lawn where guests may picnic among wildflowers. In addition, a generous continental breakfast is served in the Early American common room.

The Smiths extend a warm welcome to wine lovers, and to weary travelers.

Wine Country Inn, 1152 Lodi Lane, St. Helena 94574. Telephone (707) 963-7077. Rates: $80.00 - $116.00 includes continental breakfast for two. No children, no pets. No Phones. Open daily except December 22-27. Reservations suggested. Number of rooms 25.

Travel Notes: _____

_____

_____

BOTHE-NAPA VALLEY STATE PARK
Campground

The park offers camping, picnicking, and swimming (lifeguard on duty throughout the summer season). A number of hiking trails in the 1242-acre park wind off into the surrounding hills whose elevations reach 2000 feet. A variety of native fauna can be observed by the watchful hiker among the stands of coastal redwood and forests of Douglas fir, oak, Madrone, and other native trees.

There are fifty campsites on the grounds, each with table and barbecue. Restrooms with hot water showers and laundry tubs are nearby.

Bothe-Napa Valley State Park, 3601 St. Helena Hwy., Calistoga 94515. Telephone (707) 942-4575. Price: $5.00 - $6.00/night, $2.00/day. Reservations recommended. Number of campsites: 50. Tickets available by Ticketron.

THE BALE MILL INN   *Inn*

The Bale Mill Inn lies just north of the town of St. Helena directly on Highway 29. A rustic antique shop of the same name fills the building's lower floor while upstairs, the Inn offers five guest rooms with two shared baths. Each room is themed around a legendary person, who is characterized by its furnishings and accessories. A sitting room provides an amiable setting for guests to sip Chardonnay with which innkeeper Tom Scheibal greets them. The room's view through French doors is of the log cabin Tom built for himself and his young son. Each morning at the Inn begins with a breakfast of freshly baked cinnamon bread, warming in the sitting room's antique oven, pastries, fresh squeezed orange juice and coffee.

Bale Mill Inn, 3431 N. St. Helena Hwy., St. Helena 94574. Telephone (707) 963-4545. Rates: $55.00 - $60.00. Cards: MC, VISA. Number of rooms: 5.

MOUNTAIN HOME RANCH   *Resort, Restaurant*

Ludwig and Emma Orth homesteaded this isolated mountain resort in 1913. The first guests slept in candlelit tents and ate on the back porch in the proprietor's home. Today guests can choose their accommodations from very rustic summer cabins to modern cottages.

Mountain Home Ranch offers a leisurely vacation setting amid 350 forested acres. Trails meander along the foothills where guests will find a redwood-shaded creek and a lake for fishing. Recreational facilities include swimming pools and a tennis court.

Mountain Home Ranch, Mountain Home Ranch Road, Calistoga 94515. Telephone (707) 942-6616. Hours: Friday, Saturday 6:00 - 10:00 p.m.; Sunday 4:00 - 8:00 p.m. Price Range: $5.60 - $14.00. Corkage: $2.00. Room rates: American plan: $25.00 - $53.00 single, $45.00 - $75.00 double; European plan: $30.00 - $40.00 single, $38.00 - 45.00 double. Reservations suggested. Cards: BA, MC. Number of rooms: 26.

CALISTOGA SPA   *Spa, Motel*

Two outdoor mineral pools at the Calistoga Spa are open to the public from 8:30 a.m. to 9:00 p.m. every day of the year. The open air pool is 100° F; the other is a 105° F covered octagonal pool with benches, whirlpool jets and a cool water fountain. The pools are surrounded by garden greenery and lounge chairs perfect for relaxing on starlit summer evenings. Some how, the night-time ambience here seems almost tropical.

The indoor bath facilities are similar to those found in other Calistoga spas. Available are mud bath, whirlpool, steam, blanket sweat and massage. In addition an outdoor Olympic-size pool (85°) is open to the public during the summer from 11:00 a.m. - 8:00 p.m.

All of the forty-one rooms at the spa are of very recent construction with spacious wood-panelled interiors and open beam ceilings. All rooms are equipped for light housekeeping with kitchenettes. Guests have free use of both the outdoor hot pools and the large cooler pool when open.

Calistoga Spa, 1006 Washington St., Calistoga 94515. Telephone (707) 942-6269. Rates: Single from $32.00, Double from $42.00. Treatments available: mud bath with mineral tub, steam room and blanket wrap $16.00; with massage $30.00. Reservations suggested. Cards: BA, MC. Number of rooms: 41.

DR. WILKINSON'S HOT SPRINGS   *Spa, Motel*

"The Napa Valley with its wine grapes and health spas is a very European slice of life," exclaims Dr. Wilkinson, who established this hot springs here twenty-eight years ago.

Once in the lobby of Dr. Wilkinson's spa, one gets the distinct impression of being in a private European medical clinic. Attendants are on hand to offer assistance with the available treatments: Whirlpool, mineral tub, hot mud bath, massage. Near the bath house is an indoor hot mineral pool, equipped with hydrojets.

Rooms are available for daily or weekly stays in units that fulfill all the requirements for quality modern motel accommodations, including color cable television and air-conditioning. Rooms with kitchens are also available for an additional nightly charge of $5.00. Guests have use of the indoor mineral whirlpool for $1.00 daily charge. There is also an outdoor swimming pool for motel guests.

Dr. Wilkinson's Hot Springs, 1507 Lincoln Ave., Calistoga 94515. Telephone (707) 942-4102 or 942-6257. Rates: Single $36.00 - $41.00, Double $40.00 - $57.00. Treatments available: mud bath, mineral whirlpool bath with steam room, blanket wrap $22.00; massage with whirlpool mineral bath $27.00; mud bath, whirlpool mineral bath, steam room, blanket wrap and massage $34.00; massage only $15.00. Cards: VISA, MC. Motel reservations and bath appointments recommended. Number of rooms: 36.

Travel Notes: _____

_____

_____

NANCE'S HOT SPRINGS *Spa, Motel*

Charles Nance worked at the Pacteteau Hot Springs until 1917, then built his own spa on an adjoining piece of property, with the help of partner Frank Hughes. Today, Hughes' son, Frank, Jr., and wife, Cathy, run the family business with the help of their children. Familiar faces return year after year to enjoy the healthful waters.

The spa facilities at Nance's date back sixty years and offer the traditional mud bath, mineral tub, sulphur steam cabinet, massage and blanket sweat.

Nance's Hot Springs, 1614 Lincoln Ave., Calistoga 94515. Telephone (707) 942-6211. Hours: 8:30 - 3:30 daily. Bath combinations: mud, mineral bath, steam and blanket sweat, $18.00; with massage, $28.00; mineral bath, steam and blanket sweat, $12.00; with massage $23.00; massage $16.00. Room rates: $33.00 single: $36.00 double. Cards: BA, MC.

GOLDEN HAVEN *Motel, Spa*

The Golden Haven is located in a quiet residential section, three blocks from Calistoga's main street, and a few minutes' walk from the city's tennis courts. The twenty-six room complex has a very modern appearance.

All guests have use of the naturally heated indoor mineral pool (80 degrees) and sunken bubble pool (100 degrees). It is a short stroll to a separate building at the end of the drive where couples may enjoy the only private jacuzzi whirlpool bath in Calistoga.

Golden Haven, 1713 Lake Street, Calistoga 94515. Telephone (707) 942-6793. Room rates: $36.00 single, $45.00 double. Open daily. Treatments: intensive massage, ½ hour $16.00, 1 hour $28.00. Foot reflexology $16.00; private jacuzzi bath ½ hour $5.00; mud bath $18.00. Cards: VISA, MC. Number of rooms 30. Reservations recommended.

PACHETEAU'S HOT SPRINGS *Spa, Lodging*

This venerable establishment rests on the site of Sam Brannan's original bath houses. Century-old palms line the circular drive through the grounds. The Pacheteau family acquired this property from Senator Leland Stanford sixty years ago, and the present bath facilities date back to that period. In the central lobby, guests are segregated—men to the left, women to the right—and led to the bath quarters from which wafts the distinct sulphur smell of the vaporous waters. Available are sulphur steam cabinet, hot mineral tub, mud bath (prepared from the black volcanic ash on the grounds) and massage, as well as a 90% mineral water outdoor Olympic-sized pool (April-October).

There are twelve housekeeping cottages on the grounds. Each unit has three very clean rooms including a bedroom with twin beds, a full kitchen and a bathroom with shower. The cottages are quite far apart and a good distance from the road giving a feeling of seclusion and privacy. Overnight guests have free use of the pool.

Pacheteau's Calistoga Hot Springs, 1712 Lincoln Ave., Calistoga 94515. Telephone (707) 942-5589. Bath hours: 8:00 a.m. - 3:00 p.m. daily. Treatments: mud bath with mineral tub, sulphur steam, blanket wrap, $12.00, with massage, $24.00; steam bath with mineral tub, blanket wrap, $9.00; with massage $21.00; massage and shower, $15.00. Outdoor pool, $3.50/day, 10:00 - 6:00. Room rates: $30.00 single or double. Cards: BA, MC. Reservations recommended. Number of rooms 12.

MOUNT VIEW *Hotel, Restaurant*

The old, somewhat decaying Mount View Hotel has been stunningly revitalized. The decor bears a fairly strong 1930's influence, and with the exception of the bar, is quite convincing. The rooms are somewhat small, but nicely appointed; the suites are larger and rather elaborately furnished, bearing eclectic themes, like the "Tom Mix" room.

The Mount View has become quite the popular watering hole with the locals who drift between here, the Silverado, and the Calistoga Inn—all in easy walking distance.

The owners have sacked numerous chefs and staff members in their quest for a superior restaurant, and it must be said that the cuisine is steadily improving. Both a la carte and prix-fixe meals are served in the elegantly appointed dining room.

Mount View Hotel & Restaurant, 1457 Lincoln Ave., Calistoga 94515. Telephone (707) 942-6877. Restaurant hours: continental breakfast for guests 7:00 - 10:00 a.m., Breakfast Saturday 8:00 a.m. - 11:00 a.m., Sunday brunch 9:00 a.m. - 2:00 p.m. Dinner Monday - Saturday 6:00 - 10:00 p.m., Sunday 6:30 p.m. - 9:30 p.m. Bar open until 2:00 a.m. Price range: breakfast, from $5.00; dinner, from $11.00. Hotel rates: rooms, $45.00 - $75.00; suites, $90.00 - $125.00. Number of rooms: 25; suites: 9. Cards: MC, VISA, AE, DC. Reservations suggested.

ROMAN SPA *Spa, Lodging*

The Roman Spa, formerly Piner's Hot Springs, has undergone a facelift at the hands of new owners Max and Gena Quast. The old and the new facilities coexist here in democratic fashion with the rates based on the age of the accommodations. New units have color T.V.s and full kitchens. Original units have cooktop stoves only.

Roman Spa, 1300 Washington St., Calistoga 94515. Telephone - Motel (707) 942-4441, Spa (707) 942-6122. Treatments: jacuzzi and massage, $30.00; 60 minute massage, $26.00; thirty minute massage, $16.00; acupressure massage, $26.00; foot reflexology (includes herbal footbath), $24.00; herbal facial with clay mask, $24.00; herbal blanket sweat and mineral bath, $12.00. Room rates: new units, $42.00 - $74.00 double; old units, $32.00 - $35.00 double.

The
Wineries

ACACIA WINERY
Address: 2750 Los Amigos Rd., Napa 94559
Phone: (707) 226-9991
Hours: not open to the public
Facilities: None
Winemaker: Larry Brooks
Vineyards: 50 acres
Volume: 22,000

ALTA VINEYARD CELLAR
Address: 1311 Schramsberg Rd., Calistoga 94515
Phone: (707) 942-6708
Hours: Visitors by appt. only
Facilities: Retail Sales
Winemaker: Jon P. Axhelm
Vineyards: 10 acres
Volume: 2,000 cases

S. ANDERSON VINEYARD
Address: 1473 Yountville Crossroad, Napa
Phone: (707) 944-8642
Hours: visitors by appt. only
Facilities: tours & tasting by appt. only
Winemaker: Stanley Anderson
Vineyards: 50 acres
Volume: 4,000 cases

BEAULIEU VINEYARD
Address: 1960 St. Helena Hwy, Rutherford 94573
Phone: (707) 963-1451
Hours: 10 - 4 daily
Facilities: tours, tasting, sales
Winemaker: Thomas B. Selfridge
Vineyards: 1500 acres
Volume: 300,000 cases

BERINGER VINEYARDS
 Address: 2000 Main St., St. Helena 94574
 Phone: (707) 963-7115
 Hours: 9-4:45 daily, tours 9:30-3:45, Mem. Day - Oct. 10-6
 Facilities: tasting, tours, sales, gifts
 Winemaker: Myron S. Nightingale
 Vineyards: 2800 acres
 Volume: 275,000 cases

BUEHLER VINEYARDS
 Address: 820 Greenfield Rd., St. Helena 94574
 Phone: (707) 963-2155
 Hours: no tours, no appt.
 Facilities: none - closed to public
 Winemaker: Heidi Peterson
 Vineyards: 60 acres
 Volume: 5,000 cases

BURGESS CELLARS
 Address: 1108 Deer Park Rd., St. Helena 94574
 Phone: (707) 963-4766
 Hours: 10-4 daily
 Facilities: retail sales, tours by appt.
 Winemaker: Bill Sorenson
 Vineyards: 70 acres
 Volume: 25,000 cases

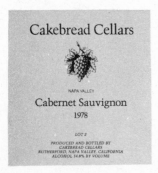

CAKEBREAD CELLARS
 Address: 8300 St. Helena Hwy., Rutherford 94573
 Phone: (415)832-8444
 Hours: Retail sales 10 - 4
 Facilities: Tours by appt. only
 Winemaker: Bruce Cakebread
 Vineyards: 34 acres
 Volume: 10,000 cases

CALAFIA WINES
    Address: 629 Fulton Ln., St. Helena 94574
    Phone: (707) 963-0114
    Hours: by appt. only
    Facilities: retail sales, no tasting
    Winemaker: Randle Johnson
    Vineyards: none
    Volume: 2,000 cases

CALIF. MEADERY/WINERY OF THE ROSES
    Address: P.O. Box 235, Napa 94559
    Phone: (707) 253-7280
    Hours: not open to the public
    Facilities: none
    Winemaker: Bruce H. Rector
    Vineyards: none
    Volume: Honeywine (Mead) 900 cases, wine 900 cases

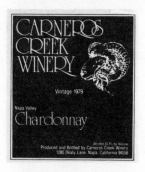

CARNEROS CREEK WINERY
    Address: 1285 Deally Lane, Napa
    Phone: (707) 253-WINE (9463)
    Hours: Mon.-Fri. 10-4
    Facilities: sales, tours by appt. only
    Winemaker: Francis Mahoney
    Vineyards: 30 acres
    Volume: 20,000 cases

CASA NUESTRA
    Address: 3473 Silverado Trail N., St. Helena 94574
    Phone: (707) 963-4684
    Hours: by invitation
    Facilities:
    Winemaker: Allen Price
    Vineyards: 10 acres
    Volume: 1,000 cases

CASSAYRE-FORNI CELLARS
Address: 1271 Manley Lane, Rutherford 94573
Phone: (707) 944-2165 or 255-0909
Hours: limited
Facilities: sales, tours by appt. only
Winemaker: Mike Forni
Vineyards: none
Volume: 5,000

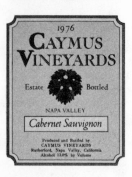

CAYMUS VINEYARDS
Address: 8700 Conn Creek Rd., Rutherford 94573
Phone: (707) 963-4204
Hours: by appt. only
Facilities: tasting and tours by appt. only
Winemakers: Charles Wagner, Randall Dunn
Vineyards: 70 acres
Volume: 34,000 cases

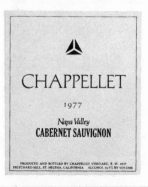

CHAPPELLET VINEYARD
Address: 1581 Sage Canyon Rd., St. Helena 94574
Phone: (707) 963-7136
Hours: tours on Friday - 1:00 by appt. only
Facilities: sales by mailing list only
Winemaker: Cathy Corison
Vineyards: 110 acres
Volume: 25,000 cases

CHATEAU BOSWELL WINERY
Address: 3468 Silverado Trail, St. Helena 94574
Phone: (707) 963-5472
Hours: visitors by appt. only
Facilities: sales, tours by appt.
Winemaker: Consultant:Andre Tchelistcheff
Vineyards: none
Volume 2,000 cases

CHATEAU BOUCHAINE
  Address: 1075 Buchli Station Rd., Napa
  Phone: (707) 252-9065
  Hours: visitors by appt. only
  Facilities: no tasting, tours by appt.
  Winemaker: Jerry Luper
  Vineyards: 30 acres
  Volume: 20,000 cases

CHATEAU CHEVALIER WINERY
  Address: 3101 Spring Mtn. Rd., St. Helena 94574
  Phone: (707) 963-2342
  Hours: not open to the public
  Facilities: by appt. only
  Winemaker: Greg Bissonette
  Vineyards: 60 acres
  Volume: 10,000 cases

CHATEAU CHEVRE WINERY
  Address: 2040 Hoffman Ln., Yountville
  Phone: (70) 944-2184
  Hours: by appt. only
  Facilities: by appt. only
  Winemaker: Gerald P. Hazen
  Vineyards: 21 acres
  Volume: 1,200 cases

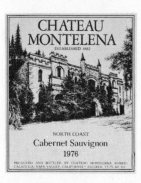

CHATEAU MONTELENA WINERY
  Address: 1429 Tubbs Ln., Calistoga 94515
  Phone: (707) 942-5105
  Hours: 10-4 Daily
  Facilities: retail sales, tours by appt.
  Winemaker: Bo Barrett
  Vineyards: 90 acres
  Volume: 25,000 cases

THE CHRISTIAN BROTHERS
WINE AND CHAMPAGNE CELLARS/MONT LA SALLE
Address 2555 North Main St., St. Helena 94574
Phone: (707) 963-2719
Hours: 10-4:30 daily/Mont La Salle closed to the public
Facilities: tours, tasting, sales
Winemaker: Brother Timothy
Vineyards: 1300 acres
Volume: (storage approx. 36,000,000 gals.)

CLOS DU VAL
Address: 5330 Silverado Trail, Napa
Phone: (707) 252-6711
Hours: 9-4 weekdays; 10-4 Saturday
Facilities: sales, tours by appt. picnic tables
Winemaker: Bernard M. Portet
Vineyards: 200 acres
Volume: 25,000

CONN CREEK WINERY
Address: 8711 Silverado Trail, St. Helena 94574
Phone: (707) 963-5133 or 963-9100
Hours: Not open to the public
Facilities: tours and tasting by appt. only
Winemaker: Daryl Eklund
Vineyards: 150 acres
Volume: 20,000 cases

CUVAISON
Address: 4550 Silverado Trail, Calistoga 94515
Phone: (707) 942-6266
Hours: 10-4, Wed.-Sun. Summer; daily
Facilities: sales, tasting
Winemaker: John Thacher
Vineyards: 400 acres
Volume: 20,000 cases annually

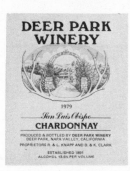

DEER PARK WINERY
   Address: 1000 Deer Park Rd., Deer Park
   Phone: (707) 963-5411
   Hours: tours by appt. only
   Facilities: sales; picnics by appt.
   Winemaker: David Clark
   Vineyards: 7 acres
   Volume: 5,000 cases

DIAMOND CREEK VINEYARDS
   Address 1500 Diamond Mtn. Rd., Calistoga 94515
   Phone: (707) 942-6926
   Hours: not open to the public
   Facilities: not open to the public
   Winemaker: Al Brounstein
   Vineyards: 20 acres
   Volume: 2,000 cases

DOMAINE CHANDON
   Address: California Drive, Yountville 94599
   Phone: (707) 944-2280
   Hours: 11-5:30 daily May - Oct.; Wed.-Sun. Nov.-Apr.
   Facilities: tasting, tours, sales, restaurant
   Winemakers: Edmond Maudiere (Moet & Chandon, France)
                and Dawnine Sample Dyer
   Vineyards: 1,500 acres
   Volume: 180,000 cases

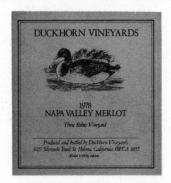

DUCKHORN VINEYARDS
   Address: 3027 Silverado Trail, St. Helena 94574
   Phone: (707) 963-7108
   Hours: sales 9 to 5 daily
   Facilities: no tasting, tours
   Winemaker: Thomas Rinaldi
   Vineyards: 6.5 acres
   Volume: 2,500 cases annually

DUNN VINEYARDS
    Address: 805 White Cottage Rd., Angwin
    Phone: (707) 965-3642
    Hours: by appt. only
    Facilities: by appt. only
    Winemaker: Randall Dunn
    Vineyards: 6 acres
    Volume: 1,000 cases

EVENSEN VINEYARDS & WINERY
    Address: 8254 St. Helena Hwy., Oakville
    Phone: (707) 944-2396
    Hours: visitors by appt. only
    Facilities: none
    Winemaker: Richard Evensen
    Vineyards: 20 acres
    Volume: 800 cases

FAR NIENTE WINERY
    Address: P.O. Box 327, Oakville
    Phone: (707) 944-2861
    Hours: visitors by appt. only; members of trade only
    Facilities: by appt. only
    Winemaker: Gil Nickel
    Vineyards: 100 acres
    Volume: 12,00 cases

FLORA SPRINGS WINE COMPANY
    Address: 1978 W. Zinfandel Ln., St. Helena 94574
    Phone: (707) 963-5711
    Hours: 8-4:30
    Facilities: no facilities for the public
    Winemaker: Ken Deis
    Vineyards: 235 acres
    Volume: 10,000 cases

FRANCISCAN VINEYARDS
   Address 1178 Galleron Rd., Rutherford 94573
   Phone: (707) 963-7111
   Hours: 10-5 daily
   Facilities: tasting, tours, sales, gifts
   Winemaker: Thomas Ferrell
   Vineyards: 500 acres
   Volume: 100,000 cases

FREEMARK ABBEY WINERY
   Address: 3022 St. Helena Hwy., St. Helena 94574
   Phone: (707) 963-9694
   Hours: 10:30-4:30 daily
   Facilities: tours (at 2 p.m. daily), sales, gifts
   Winemaker: Larry Langbehn
   Vineyards: 130 acres
   Volume: 25,000

**LABEL NOT
AVAILABLE
AT PRESS TIME**

FROG'S LEAP WINERY
   Address: 3358 St. Helena Hwy., St. Helena 94574
   Phone: (707) 963-4704
   Hours: by appt. only
   Facilities: by appt. only
   Winemaker: John Williams
   Vineyards: 10 acres
   Volume 2,000 cases

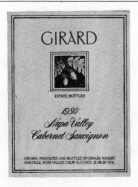

GIRARD
   Address: 7717 Silverado Trail, Oakville
   Phone: (707) 944-8577
   Hours: by appt. only
   Facilities: sales-tours & tasting by appt.
   Winemaker: Fred Payne
   Vineyards: 44 acres
   Volume: 14.000 cases

GREEN & RED VINEYARD
Address: 3208 Chiles Pope Valley Rd., St. Helena 94574
Phone: (707) 965-2346
Hours: by appt. only
Facilities: by appt. only
Winemaker: Jay Heminway
Vineyards: 16 acres
Volume: 1,500 cases

GRGICH HILLS CELLARS
Address: 1829 St. Helena Hwy., Rutherford
Phone: (707) 963-2784
Hours: sales 10-4 daily
Facilities: tours by appt.; no tasting
Winemaker: Miljenko ''Mike'' Grgich
Vineyards: 140 acres
Volume: 20,000 cases

HEITZ WINE CELLARS
Address: 500 Taplin Rd., St. Helena 94574
Phone: (707) 963-3542
Hours: 11-4:30 at 436 St. Helena Hwy.
Facilities: tasting, Mon.-Fri.; sales daily
Winemaker: Joe and David Heitz
Vineyards: 50 acres
Volume: 40,000 cases

WILLIAM HILL WINERY
Address: P.O. Box 3989, Napa
Phone: (707) 224-6565
Hours: not open to the public
Facilities: none
Winemaker: William Hill
Vineyards: 700 acres
Volume: 22,000 cases

HNW CELLARS
   Address: P.O. Box 153 - 850 Rutherford Rd., Rutherford 94573
   Phone: (707) 963-5618
   Hours: Call for Appt.
   Facilities: Call for appt.
   Vineyards 67 acres
   Volume: Not available

INGLENOOK VINEYARDS
   Address: 1991 St. Helena Hwy., Rutherford 94573
   Phone: (707) 963-7184
   Hours: 10-5 daily
   Facilities: tasting, tours, sales, museum
   Winemaker: John Richburg
   Vineyards: 2,800 acres
   Volume: 4,500,000 cases annually

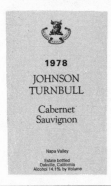

JOHNSON TURNBULL VINEYARDS
   Address: 8210 St. Helena Hwy., Oakville
   Phone: (707) 963-5389 or (415) 563-0807
   Hours: by appt. only
   Facilities: not open to the public
   Winemaker-Consultant: Lawrence Wara
   Vineyards: 21 acres
   Volume: 1200 cases

ROBERT KEENAN WINERY
   Address: 3660 Spring Mtn. Rd., St. Helena 94574
   Phone: (707) 963-9177
   Hours: not open to the public
   Facilities: by appt. only
   Winemaker: Joe Cafaro
   Vineyards: 43 acres
   Volume: 8,000 cases

HANNS KORNELL CHAMPAGNE CELLARS
Address: 1091 Larkmead Lane, St. Helena
Phone: (707) 963-2334
Hours: 10-4 daily
Facilities: tasting, tours, sales, gifts
Champagne Producer: Hanns Kornell
Vineyards: none
Volume: 125,000 cases

CHARLES KRUG/CK MONDAVI
Address: 2800 Main St., St. Helena
Phone: (707) 963-2761
Hours: 10-4 daily
Facilities: tours, tasting, sales
Winemaker: Peter Mondavi
Vineyards: 1,200 acres
Volume: 1,500,000 cases annually

LAKESPRING WINERY
Address: 2055 Hoffman Ln., Napa
Phone: (707) 944-2475
Hours: 8-4 daily
Facilities: no tours or tasting
Winemaker: Randy Mason
Vineyards: 8 acres
Volume: 15,000 cases

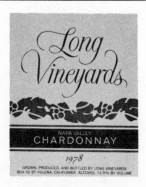

LONG VINEYARDS
Address: Box 50, St. Helena
Phone: (707) 963-2496
Hours: by appt. only
Facilities: no tours, no tasting
Winemaker: Bob Long
Vineyards: 15 acres
Volume: 1,000 cases

MARKHAM WINERY
   Address: 2812 N. St. Helena Hwy., St. Helena
   Phone: (707) 963-5292
   Hours: 11-4 daily; sensory evaluation daily 11:30
   Facilities: tasting, sales, and tours by appt.
   Winemaker: Robert D. Foley
   Vineyards: 264 acres
   Volume: 18,000 cases

LOUIS M. MARTINI
   Address: 254 St. Helena Hwy. So., St. Helena 94574
   Phone: (707) 963-2736
   Hours: 10-4:30 daily
   Facilities: tasting, tours, sales
   Winemaker: Louis P. & Michael R. Martini
   Vineyards: 1,000 acres
   Volume: 320,000 cases

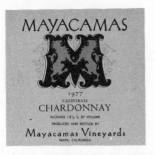

MAYACAMAS VINEYARDS
   Address: 1155 Lokoya Rd., Napa
   Phone: (707) 224-4030
   Hours: by appt. only
   Facilities: tours & sales by appt. only
   Winemaker: Bob Travers
   Vineyards: 45 acres
   Volume: 5,000 cases annually

LOUIS K. MILHALY VINEYARD
   Address: 3103 Silverado Trail, Napa
   Phone: (707) 253-9306
   Hours: not open to public
   Facilities: none
   Winemaker: John O. Nemeth
   Vineyards: 34 acres
   Volume: 12,000 cases

LABEL NOT
AVAILABLE
AT PRESS TIME

F. J. MILLER
  Address: 8329 St. Helena Hwy., Napa
  Phone: (707) 963-4252
  Hours: by appt. only
  Facilities: by appt. only
  Winemaker: F. Justin Miller
  Vineyards: none
  Volume: research & development

ROBERT MONDAVI WINERY
  Address: 7801 St. Helena Hwy., Oakville
  Phone: (707) 963-9611
  Hours: 10 to 5 daily
  Facilities: tours, including tasting; sales
  Winemaker: Robert & Tim Mondavi
  Vineyards: 1094 acres

MONT ST. JOHN CELLARS
  Address: 5400 Old Sonoma Rd., Napa
  Phone: (707) 255-8864
  Hours 10-4 daily
  Facilities: wine tasting
  Winemaker: Andrea Bartolucci
  Vineyards: 160 acres
  Volume: 10,000 cases

MT. VEEDER WINERY
  Address: 1999 Mt. Veeder Rd., Napa
  Phone: (707) 224-4039
  Hours: none
  Facilities: tours or weekdays by prior appt.
  Winemaker: Peter Franus
  Vineyards: 20 acres
  Volume: 5,000 cases

NAPA CREEK WINERY
    Address: 1001 Silverado Trail, St. Helena
    Phone: (707) 963-9456
    Hours: 8:30-5 daily
    Facilities: tours by appt., case sales
    Winemaker: Jack Schulze
    Vineyards: none
    Volume: 10,000 cases

NAPA WINE CELLARS
    Address: 7481 St. Helena Hwy., Oakville
    Phone: (707) 944-2565
    Hours: 10:30-5:30 daily
    Facilities: tasting, sales, self guided tour
    Winemaker: Aaron Mosley
    Vineyards: 3 acres
    Volume: 14,000 cases

NEWLAN VINEYARDS & WINERY
    Address: 5225 St. Helena Hwy., Napa
    Phone: (707) 944-2914
    Hours: visitors by appt. only
    Facilities: tours by appt. only
    Winemaker: Bruce M. Newlan
    Vineyards: 60 acres
    Volume: 3,000 cases

NEWTON WINERY
    Address: not available
    Phone: (707) 963-4613
    Hours: not open to public
    Facilities: not open to the public
    Winemaker: not available
    Vineyards: 100 acres
    Volume: 13,00 cases

NICHELINI VINEYARDS
Address: 2349 Lower Chiles Valley Rd., St. Helena
Phone: (707) 963-3357
Hours: 10-6 Sat.-Sun., Mon.-Fri. by appt. only
Facilities: tours, tasting, sales, picnics
Winemaker: Jim Nichelini
Vineyards: 70 acres
Volume: 8,000 cases

LABEL NOT
AVAILABLE
AT PRESS TIME

NIEBAUM-COPPOLA ESTATE
Address: 1460 Niebaum Lane, Rutherford
Phone: (707) 963-9435
Hours: call for appt.
Facilities: tours by appt. only
Winemaker: Russ Turner
Vineyards: 110 acres
Volume: 4,000 cases

ROBERT PECOTA WINERY
Address: 3299 Bennett Lane, Calistoga
Phone: (707) 942-6625
Hours: by appt. only
Facilities: by appt. only
Winemaker: Bob Pecota
Vineyards: 35 acres
Volume: 10,000 cases

ROBERT PEPI WINERY
Address: 7585 St. Helena Hwy., P.O. Box 421, Oakville
Phone: (707) 944-2807
Hours: visitors by appt. only, 2:30 Tues.-Thur.
Facilities: no tasting, tours by appt. only
Winemaker: Bob Pepi
Vineyards: 70 acres
Volume: 16,000

JOSEPH PHELPS VINEYARDS
   Address: 200 Taplin Rd., Box 1031, St. Helena
   Phone: (707) 963-2745
   Hours: Mon.-Fri. 8-5 by appt.; Sat. 10-4:30 by appt.
   Facilities: sales; tours, tasting by appt.
   Winemaker: Walter Schug
   Vineyards: 175 acres
   Volume: 55,000 cases

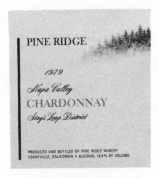

PINE RIDGE WINERY
   Address: 5901 Silverado Trail, Napa
   Phone: (707) 253-7500
   Hours: Wed.-Sun. 11-3:30
   Facilities: tasting, picnic area, tours by appt.
   Winemaker: Gary Andrus
   Vineyards: 125 acres
   Volume: 15,000 cases

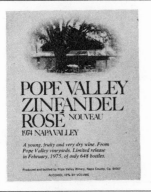

POPE VALLEY WINERY
   Address: 6613 Pope Valley Rd., Pope Valley
   Phone: (707) 965-2192
   Hours: weekends after 11:00
   Facilities: tasting, sales
   Winemaker: Steve Devitt
   Vineyards: 1 acre
   Volume: 10,000 cases

PRAGER WINERY & PORT WORKS
   Address: 1281 Lewellng Ln., St. Helena
   Phone: (707) 963-3720
   Hours: by appt. only
   Facilities: by appt. only
   Winemaker: Jim Prager
   Vineyards: ½ acres
   Volume: 2,000 cases

QUAIL RIDGE
Address: 1055 Atlas Peak Rd., Napa
Phone: (707) 944-8128
Hours: visitors by appt. only
Facilities: tours & sales by appt.
Winemaker: Elaine Wellesley & Leon Santoro
Vineyards: 20 acres
Volume: 5,800 cases

RAYMOND VINEYARD AND CELLAR
Address: 849 Zinfandel Lane, St. Helena
Phone: (707) 963-3141
Hours: by appt. only
Facilities: tasting, tours, sales by appt.
Winemaker: Walter Raymond
Vineyards: 80 acres
Volume: 40,000 cases

RITCHIE CREEK VINEYARD
Address: 4024 Spring Mtn. Rd., St. Helena
Phone: (707) 963-4661
Hours: by appt. only
Facilities: tours, sales by appt.
Winemaker: Pete Minor
Vineyards: 10 acres
Volume: 400 cases

RODDIS CELLAR
Address: 1510 Diamond Mtn. Rd., Calistoga
Phone: (707) 942-5868
Hours: 9-5 daily
Facilities: tasting and tours by appt. only
Winemaker: William H. Roddis
Vineyards: 3½ acres
Volume: 500 cases

DON CHARLES ROSS WINERY
    Address: 1721 -C- Action Ave., Napa
    Phone: (707) 255-9463
    Hours: not open to the public
    Facilities: by appt. only
    Winemaker: Don Ross
    Vineyards: none
    Volume: 5,000 cases

ROUND HILL VINEYARDS
    Address: 1097 Lodi Lane, St. Helena
    Phone: (707) 963-5251
    Hours: 9-5 weekdays, 11-5 weekends
    Facilities: tours by appt. only
    Winemaker: Charles Abela
    Vineyards: none
    Volume: 60,000 cases

RUTHERFORD HILL WINERY
    Address: Rutherford Hill Rd., Rutherford
    Phone: (707) 963-9694
    Hours: 10:30-4:30 daily
    Facilities: tasting, tours, sales
    Winemaker: Phil Baxter
    Vineyards: none - partners vineyards
    Volume: 85,000 cases

RUTHERFORD VINTNERS
    Address: 1673 St. Helena Hwy. So., Rutherford
    Phone: (707) 963-4117
    Hours: 10-4:30 daily
    Facilities: tasting, sales, gifts
    Winemaker: Bernard L. Skoda
    Vineyards: 30 acres
    Volume: 15,000 cases

SAGE CANYON WINERY
  Address: P.O. Box 458, Rutherford 94573
  Phone: (415) 664-8721
  Hours: visitors by appt. only
  Facilities: visitors by appt. only
  Winemaker-Consultant: Charles Ortman
  Vineyard: none
  Volume: 1300 cases

ST. ANDREWS WINERY
  Address: 2921 Silverado Trail, Napa
  Phone: (707) 252-6748
  Hours: by appt. only
  Facilities: by appt. only
  Winemaker: Chuck Ortman
  Vineyards: 65 acres
  Volume: 5,000 cases

ST. CLEMENT VINEYARDS
  Address: 2867 St. Helena Hwy. No., St. Helena
  Phone: (707) 963-7221
  Hours: by appt. only
  Facilities: sales in case lots only
  Winemakers: William J. Casey & Dennis Johns
  Vineyards: 2 acres
  Volume: 9,000 cases

V. SATTUI WINERY
  Address: White Lane, St. Helena
  Phone: (707) 963-7774
  Hours: 9-6 daily Mar.-Nov., 9-5 Dec.-Feb.
  Facilities: tasting, sales, cheese shop, gifts
  Winemaker: Daryl Sattui
  Vineyards: none
  Volume: 8,000 cases

SCHRAMSBERG VINEYARDS
Address: Schramsberg Rd., Calistoga
Phone: (707) 942-4558
Hours: by appointment
Facilities: tours, sales
Winemaker: Gregory Fowler
Vineyards: 40 acres
Volume: 25,000 cases annually

SEQUOIA GROVE VINEYARDS
Address: 8338 St. Helena Hwy., Rutherford
Phone: (707) 944-2945
Hours: 11-5 by appt. only
Facilities: tasting, sales, tours
Winemaker: James W. Allen
Vineyards: 24 acres
Volume: 6,300 cases

SHAFER VINEYARDS
Address: 6154 Silverado Trail, Napa
Phone: (707) 944-2877
Hours: by appt. only
Facilities: winery
Winemaker: Nikko Schoch
Vineyards: 60 acres
Volume: 15,000 cases

CHARLES F. SHAW VINEYARD & WINERY
Address: 1010 Big Tree Road, St. Helena
Phone: (707) 963-5459
Hours: by appt. only
Facilities: tasting, tours, sales by appt.
Winemaker: Richard W. Forman
Vineyards: 48 acres
Volume: 15,000 cases

SHOWN & SONS VINEYARDS
  Address: 8643 Silverado Trail, Rutherford
  Phone: (707) 963-9004
  Hours: 10-4 daily
  Facilities: tours, tasting, sales
  Winemaker: James Vahl
  Vineyards: 75 acres
  Volume: 12,000 cases annually

SILVERADO VINEYARDS
  Address: 6121 Silverado Trail, Napa
  Phone: (707) 257-1770
  Hours: not open to the public
  Facilities: not open to the public
  Winemaker: John Stuart
  Vineyards: 185 acres
  Volume: 45,000 cases

SILVER OAK CELLARS
  Address: 915 Oakville Cross Rd., Oakville
  Phone: (707) 944-8808
  Hours: tours by appt. only
  Facilities: sales; no tasting
  Winemaker: Justin Meyer
  Vineyards: 15 acres
  Volume: 13,000 cases

SMITH-MADRONE VINEYARDS
  Address: 4022 Spring Mtn. Rd., St. Helena
  Phone: (707) 963-2283
  Hours: by appointment only
  Facilities: tours, sales, tasting·
  Winemakers: Charles & Stuart Smith
  Vineyards: 38 + acres
  Volume: projected 5,000 cases annually

SPRING MOUNTAIN VINEYARDS
    Address: 2805 Spring Mt. Rd., St. Helena
    Phone: (707) 963-5233
    Hours: by appointment only
    Facilities: sales; tours by appt.
    Winemaker: John Williams
    Vineyards: 125 acres
    Volume: 25,000 cases

STAG'S LEAP WINE CELLARS
    Address: 5766 Silverado Trail, Napa
    Phone: (707) 944-2020 or 944-2782
    Hours: daily 10-4 retail sales
    Facilities: tours by appt. only
    Winemaker: Warren Winiarski
    Vineyards: 44 acres
    Volume: 20,000 cases

STAG'S LEAP WINERY
    Address: 6150 Silverado Trail, Napa
    Phone: (707) 253-1545
    Hours: none
    Facilities: none available to the public
    Winemaker: Carl Doumani
    Vineyards: 100 acres
    Volume: 9,000 cases

STERLING VINEYARDS
    Address: 1111 Dunaweal Lane, Calistoga
    Phone: (707) 942-5151
    Hours: 10:30-5 daily summer; 10:30-4:30, winter Wed.-Sun.
    Facilities: tasting, self-guided tours, sales
    Winemaker: Theo Rosenbrand
    Vineyards: 500 acres
    Volume: 72,000 cases

STONEGATE WINERY
Address: 1183 Dunaweal Lane, Calistoga
Phone: (707) 942-6500
Hours: 10-4 for sales weekdays
Facilities: tours by appt.
Winemaker: David Spaulding
Vineyards: 35 acres
Volume: 22,000 cases

STONY HILL VINEYARD
Address: P.O. Box 308, St. Helena
Phone: (707) 963-2636
Hours: by appointment only
Facilities: tours by appt. only. (No Sales)
Winemaker: Michael Chelini
Vineyards: 30 + acres
Volume: 4,000 cases annually

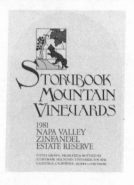

STORYBOOK MOUNTAIN VINEYARDS
Address: 3835 Highway 128, Calistoga
Phone: (707) 942-5310
Hours: by appt. only
Facilities: by appt. only
Winemaker: Dr. J. Bernard Seps
Vineyards: 36 acres
Volume: 2,500 cases

SULLIVAN VINEYARDS WINERY
Address: 1090 Galleron Lane, Rutherford
Phone: (707) 963-9646
Hours: visitors by appt. only
Facilities: by appt. only
Winemaker: James Sullivan
Vineyards: 30 acres
Volume: 1,300 cases

SUTTER HOME WINERY, INC.
  Address: 277 St. Helena Hwy. So., St. Helena
  Phone: (707) 963-3104
  Hours: 9-5 daily
  Facilities: tasting and sales
  Winemaker: Louis (Bob) Trinchero
  Vineyards: 15 acres
  Volume: 150,000 cases

TRAULSEN VINEYARDS
  Address: 2250 Lake County Hwy., Calistoga
  Phone: (707) 942-0283
  Hours: by appt. only
  Facilities: by appt. only
  Winemaker: John Traulsen
  Vineyards: 2 acres
  Volume: 500-700 cases

TREFETHEN VINEYARDS
  Address: 1160 Oak Knoll Ave., Napa
  Phone: (707) 255-7700
  Hours: by appt. only
  Facilities: by appt. only
  Winemakers: D. Whitehouse & J. Trefethen
  Vineyards: 600 acres
  Volume: 40,000 cases

TUDAL WINERY
  Address: 1015 Big Tree Rd., St. Helena
  Phone: (707) 963-3947
  Hours: not open to the public
  Facilities: by appt. only
  Winemaker: Arnold Tudal, Charles Ortman, consultant
  Vineyards: 7 acres
  Volume: 2,000 cases

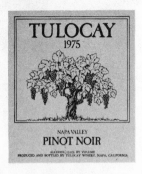

TULOCAY WINERY
    Address: P.O. Box 53, Oakville 94562;
              1426 Coombsville, Rd., Napa
    Phone: (707) 255-4064
    Hours: by appt. only
    Facilities: by appt. only
    Winemaker: W.C. Cadman
    Vineyards: none
    Volume: 2,000 cases annually

VICHON WINERY
    Address: 1595 Oakville Grade, Oakville
    Phone: (707) 944-2811
    Hours: visitors by appt. only
    Facilities: visitors by appt. only
    Winemaker: John McKay
    Vineyards: none
    Volume: 40,000 cases

VILLA MT. EDEN WINERY
    Address: 620 Oakville Crossrds., Oakville
    Phone: (707) 944-2414
    Hours: 8-5
    Facilities: tours 10-4 by appt. only
    Winemaker: Mike McGrath
    Vineyards: 87 acres
    Volume: 20,000 cases

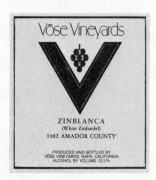

VOSE VINEYARDS
    Address: 4035 Mt. Veeder Rd., Napa
    Phone: (707) 944-2254
    Hours: daily 10-4
    Facilities: tours, sales, picnics, no tasting
    Winemaker: Hamilton Vose III
    Vineyards: 21 acres
    Volume: 17,000 cases

WHITEHALL LANE WINERY
Address: 1563 St. Helena Hwy. So., St. Helena
Phone: (707) 963-9454
Hours: 11-5 winter; 12-6 summer
Facilities: sales, tours & tasting, picnic area
Winemaker: Arthur Finkelstein
Vineyards: 23 acres
Volume: 10,000 cases

YVERDON VINEYARDS
Address: 3787 Spring Mtn. Rd., St. Helena
Phone: (707) 963-4270
Hours: not open to the public
Facilities: none available
Winemaker: Fred J. Aves
Vineyards: 92 acres
Volume: 5,000 cases annually

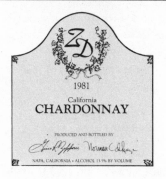

ZD WINES
Address: 8383 Silverado Trail, Napa
Phone: (707) 963-5188
Hours: 8-5, Mon.-Fri. by appt. only
Facilities: no tasting room
Winemaker: Norman de Leuze
Vineyards: 3 acres
Volume: 10,000 cases

Adventures

Napa:

Fuller Park, Jefferson & Laurel Streets, Napa
  Picnicking, playground

J.F. Kennedy Park, 2291 Napa-Vallejo Hwy. Napa
  Boating, picnicking, barbecue pits.

Napa Town & Country Fairgounds, 575 3rd St.,
  Napa
  Phone: (707) 224-7951
  Camping, showers, R.V. hook-ups.
  Admission.

Napa Valley Camping Resort, 1962 Capell Valley
  Rd., Napa (off Route 128, half-way between
  Moskowite Corners & Turtle Rock)
  Phone: (707) 226-9133
  Camping, cabins, R.V. hook-ups.
  Admission.

Oak Lake Park, 1031 La Grande Ave., Napa
  Phone: (707) 226-1133
  Swimming, picnicking, barbecue pits, horse
  shoes.
  Admission.

Skyline Park, Imola Ave. and 4th Ave. Napa
  Picnic area, camp site, museum, ball field, hiking
  trails, stream, lake, horse trails.

Summer Hill Oddfellows Park, 2202 Loma Heights
  Road, Napa.
  Phone: (707) 224-2216
  Swimming, picnicking, barbeque pits, playground
  Admission.

Yountville:

Yountville City Park, at triangular intersection of
  Washington and Lincoln St., Yountville.
  Picnicking, playground.

Rutherford:

Conn Dam Picnic Grounds, Lake Hennessey. About 3
  miles on Highway 128 after turning off Silverado
  Trail at Rutherford Cross Road.
  Picnicking, barbecue pits, fishing.

St. Helena:

Crane Park, Crane Ave., St. Helena. (Turn off Hwy.
  29 at Grayson Ave., south of town. Proceed to end
  and turn left, following signs.)
  Picnicking, barbecue pits, playground, tennis.

Lyman Park, Main Street, St. Helena. (across from the
  Post Office)
  Picnicking, fireplaces, playground.

Nichelini Vineyards, Highway 128 out past Lake
  Hennessey, St. Helena.
  Phone: (707) 963-3357
  Picnicking

V. Sattui Winery, White Lane, St. Helena.
  Picnicking & winetasting at the winery.

Calistoga:

Bothe-Napa Valley State Park, 3601 St. Helena Hwy. North, Calistoga
   Phone: (707) 942-4575
   Picnicking, campgrounds, swimming, hiking trails.
   Admission.

Calistoga Ranch Campground, 570 Lommel Road, Calistoga (off Silverado Trail).
   Phone: (707) 942-4063
   Swimming, fishing, hiking, R.V. hook-ups, camping, showers
   Admission

Chateau Montelena, 1429 Tubbs Lane, Calistoga
   Phone: (707) 942-5105
   Picnicking by prior arrangement

Napa County Fairgrounds, 1435 Oak St, Calistoga
   Phone: (707) 942-5111
   Camping, R.V. hook-ups, showers
   Admission

Pioneer Park, Cedar Street, Calistoga
   Picnicking, playground

SIGHTSEEING POSSIBILITIES

Balloon Aviation of Napa Valley
Above It All   *Hot Air Balloon Rides*
   Napa. Phone (707) 252-7067
   Rates: $95 per person, includes coffee, light brunch, wall plaque, orientation, champagne
   60 minute flight
   6 passenger maximum

Adventures Aloft   *Hot Air Balloon Rides*
   Yountville. Phone: (707) 255-8688
   Rates: $95 per person for the champagne flight; coffee and pastries
   Approximately one hour ride
   4 passenger maximum per balloon

Napa Valley Balloons, Inc.   *Hot Air Balloon Rides*
   Yountville. Phone: (707) 253-2224
   Rates: $95 - $110 per person, includes champagne, photos, picnic reception
   Approximately one hour ride
   4 passenger maximum per ballloon

PUC Flight Center   *Sightseeing Flights*
   Angwin. Phone: (707) 965-6219
   Rates: $46.50 - $57.00 per hour for up to three passengers
   Reservations required

Calistoga Soaring Center   *Glider Rides*
   1546 Lincoln Avenue, Calistoga.
   Phone (707) 942-5592
   Rates: $50 for 2 persons; $38 for 1 person
   Ride is approximately 15-20 minutes
   Reservations should be made 1 to 2 days in advance

Bridgeford Flying Service   *Sightseeing Flights*
   Napa Airport. Phone: (707) 224-0887
   Local Tour: $30 for approx. 20 minutes
   Napa Valley Tour: $50 for approx. 30 minutes
   Lake Berryessa Tour: $60 for approx. 40 mins.
   Golden Gate Tour: $75 for approx. 1 hour flight
   All prices are for the plane and the pilot — 1 to 3 passengers may fly for the fixed rate

HORSEBACK RIDING

Wild Horse Valley Ranch, Wild Horse Valley Rd., Napa 94558
   Phone: (707) 224-0727
   50 miles of trails
   Riding School, polo grounds, horse boarding
   Rates: $7/hour—trail rides; $25.00 barbecue
   $20.00 breakfast or dinner ride.

GOLF

Napa:

Napa Municipal Golf Course, 2295 Streblow Drive, Napa 94558
    Phone: (707) 255-4333
    18 holes, 6,498 yards, par 72
    Open daily

Little Knoll Golf Course, 1129 Dealy Lane, Napa 94558
    Phone: (707) 255-9781
    9 holes, 1800 yards, par 29
    Open daily

Napa Valley Country Club, 3385 Hagen Road, Napa 94558
    Phone: (707) 252-1111
    9 holes, 2,904 yards, par 36
    Closed Mondays

Silverado Country Club & Resort, 1600 Atlas Peak Road, Napa 94558
    Phone: (707) 255-2970
    18 holes, 6,117 yards, par 72
    Open daily to members and resort guests

Chimney Rock Golf Course, 5400 Silverado Trail, Napa 94558
    Phone: (707) 255-3363
    9 holes, 3,500 yards, par 36
    Open daily

St. Helena:

Meadowood Suburban Club, 900 Meadowood Lane, St. Helena 94574
    Phone: (707) 963-2752
    9 holes, 2,050 yards, par 31
    Closed Monday

Calistoga:

Mount St. Helena Golf Course, County Fairgrounds, Calistoga 94515
    Phone: (707) 942-9966
    9 holes, 2,520 yards, par 34
    Open daily

Pope Valley:

Aetna Springs Golf Course, 1600 Aetna Springs Road, Pope Valley 94567
    Phone: (707) 965-2115
    9 holes, 2,840 yards, par 35
    Open daily

TENNIS

Napa:

Vintage High School, 1375 Trower Avenue
    14 courts

Napa High School, 2475 Jefferson Street
    6 courts, 2 courts with night lighting. ?

Silverado Junior High School, 1133 Coombsville Road
    8 courts, 4 with night lighting

Redwood Junior High School, 3600 Oxford St.
    4 Courts

Ridgeview Junior High School, 2447 Old Sonoma Road
    5 courts

Napa College, Napa-Vallejo Hwy.
    8 courts

St. Helena:

Crane Park, Grayson Avenue
  2 courts

Robert Louis Stevenson School, 1316 Hillview
  Place
  2 courts

St. Helena High School, 1401 Grayson Ave.
  2 courts, night lighting.

Calistoga:

Stevenson & Grant Streets
  4 courts, night lighting

Angwin:

Pacific Union College
  6 courts, night lighting

FORMAL WINE TASTINGS

Silverado Restaurant, 1374 Lincoln Ave.,
  Calistoga 94515
  Phone: (707) 942-6725
  Every Tuesday at 7:00 p.m.
  Supervised by Alex Dierkhising

WINE TOURING SERVICES

California Wine Tours, Susan Holzhauer
  Phone: (707) 963-5205

D'Vine Wine Tours, Susan Benz
  Phone: (707) 963-2164

Grapevine Limousine
  P.O. Box 2505, Napa 94558
  Limousine rental
  Phone: (707) 255-9083

Napa Valley Double Decker Wine Tours
  Phone: (707) 255-1002

Napa Valley Vintage Tours
  Phone: (707) 253-8687

Wine Tours International

  Vintage 1870, Yountville
  Phone: (707) 224-7210

Napa County Farming Trails brochure and map; a
  listing of farms, gardens, nurseries, etc.
  where local products and produce can be
  purchased. Maps available throughout the
  valley.

Books Published by The Wine Appreciation Guild

#501 GOURMET WINE COOKING THE EASY WAY: All new recipes for memorable eating, prepared quickly and simply with wine. Most of the recipes specify convenience foods which can be delightfuly flavored with wine, enabling the busy homemaker to set a gourmet table for family and friends with a minimum of time in the kitchen. 128pp, 8½'' x 11'', illustrated, 1980 edition. $6.95 @ ISBN 0-932664-01-6.

#502 NEW ADVENTURES IN WINE COOKERY BY CALIFORNIA WINEMAKERS: Many new recipes for California's winemakers. The life work of the winemaker is to guide nature in the development in wine of beauty, aroma, bouquet and subtle flavors. These recipes contributed by Winemakers, their families and colleagues represent this spirit of flavorful good living. A best selling cookbook with 500 exciting recipes including barbecue, wine drinks, salads and sauces. 128pp, illustrated 8½'' x 11'', $6.95 @ ISBN 0-932664-10-5.

#503 FAVORITE RECIPES OF CALIFORNIA WINE-MAKERS: The original winemakers' cookbook and a bestseller for fifteen years. Over 200 dedicated winemakers, their wives and colleagues have shared with us their love of cooking. Over 500 authentic recipes, many used for generations, are included in this "cookbook classic", illustrated, $6.95 @ ISBN 0932664-03-2.

#504 DINNER MENUS WITH WINE by Emily Chase. Over 100 complete dinner menus with recommended complimentary wines. This book will make your dinner planning easy and the results impressive to your family and most sophisticated guests. 400 different recipes, and tips on serving, storing and enjoying wine. 1983 edition. 128pp, illustrated, 8½'' x 11'', $6.95 @ ISBN 0-932664-04-0.

#554 WINE CELLAR RECORD BOOK: A professionally planned, elegant, leatherette bound cellar book for the serious wine collector. Organized by the wine regions of the World, helpful for keeping perpetual inventories and monitoring the aging of each wine in your cellar. Enough space for over 200 cases of wine and spaced to record tasting notes and special events. Illustrated, 12'' x 10½'', six ring binder, additional pages available. $32.50 @ ISBN 0-932664-06-7.

#640 THE CHAMPAGNE COOKBOOK: ''Add Some Sparkle to Your Cooking and Your Life'' by Malcolm R. Herbert. Cooking with Champagne is a glamorous yet easy way to liven up your cuisine. The recipes range from soup, salads, hors d'oeuvres, fish, fowl, red meat, vegetables and of course desserts—all using Champagne. 128pp, illustrated, 8½'' x 11'' ppb, $6.95 @ ISBN 0-932664-07-5.

#641 THE POCKET ENCYCLOPEDIA OF CALIFORNIA WINE by William I. Kaufman. A convenient and thorough reference book that fits into your vest pocket and gives answers to all of your questions about California Wines. All the wineries, grape varieties, wines, geography and wine terms are covered briefly and authoritatively by one of America's foremost wine experts. Carry with you to restaurants and wine tastings to make you well informed on your choice of California Wines. 128 compact pages, 7¾'' x 3½'' with vinyl cover. $5.95 @ ISBN 0-932664-09-1, New edition.

#673 WINE IN EVERYDAY COOKING by Patti Ballard, the newest and freshest in our famous wine cookbook series. Patti is the popular wine consultant from Santa Cruz who has been impressing winery visitors and guests for years with her wine and food magic. Strong Italian heritage is evident in her recipes and the cooking tips from Patti's grandmother. Chapters range from soup and hors d'oeuvres through pasta, fish and desserts—all of course using wine. 128pp, illustrated, 8½'' x 11'' ppb, $5.95 @ ISBN 0-932664-20-2, Oct. 1981.

#671 CORKSCREWS, KEYS TO HIDDEN PLEASURES by Manfred Heckman. The first authoritative book on corkscrews, their history, science, design and enjoyment: for the connoisseur or the novice. Over 500 corkscrew models are covered with a multitude of photos and 10 full color pages. 1984 edition, $20.00, @ ISBN 0-932664-17-2.

#672 THE CALIFORNIA WINE DRINK BOOK by William I. Kaufman. Cocktails, hot drinks, punches and coolers all made with wine. Over 200 different drink recipes, using various wines along with mixing tips and wine entertaining suggestions. 128 pp, $4.95. @ ISBN 0-932664-10-9.

CALIFORNIA WINE TOURS: *"The civilized traveler's guide to the Wine Country"*. Authoritative directories of all wineries in California's major wine growing regions, complete with detailed road maps showing their exact locations, food critique on most noteworthy restaurants, review of inns, resorts, health spas, campgrounds, and "bed and breakfast" accommodations. Also a special listing of picnic areas, sightseeing possibilities, and recreation facilities.

Wine Tour of the Napa Valley - #542, $4.95

Wine Tour of Sonoma/Mendocino - #543, $4.95

Wine Tour of the Central Coast - #544, $4.95.

VINTAGEWISE: *A preview of great California wines complete with winemakers' cellar notes.* In addition to recommending the best of currently available vintages each book contains:
☆ A profile of both the winery and the winemaker.
☆ The Vintner's Notebook, including vineyard and cellar technques.
☆ The winemaker's tasting comments, in his own words.
☆ A separate page on each wine displaying a full-size label and tasting scorecard for personal use.
☆ A complete glossary and discussion of technical tasting terms.
☆ A section on sensory evaluation of wines—using the modified U.C. Davis scorecard with methods of statistical analysis.
☆ 208 pages of the best California Cabernet Sauvignons, Chardonnays, Rieslings, Sauvignon Blancs and Zinfandels. #676, $8.95.

ORDER FORM
WINE APPRECIATION GUILD
155 Connecticut Street
San Francisco, California 94107

SHIP TO:_____

Address _____

City _____ City_____Zip_____

Please send the following:

_____Copies #500 EPICUREAN RECIPES OF CALIFORNIA WINEMAKERS	$6.95	@_____
_____Copies #501 GOURMET WINE COOKING THE EASY WAY	$6.95	@_____
_____Copies #502 NEW ADVENTURES IN WINE COOKERY	$6.95	@_____
_____Copies #503 FAVORITE RECIPES OF CALIFORNIA WINEMAKERS	$6.95	@_____
_____Copies #504 DINNER MENUS WITH WINE	$6.95	@_____
_____Copies #505 EASY RECIPES OF CALIFORNIA WINEMAKERS	$6.95	@_____
_____Copies #640 THE CHAMPAGNE COOKBOOK	$6.95	@_____
_____Copies #527 IN CELEBRATION OF WINE & LIFE	$20.00	@_____
_____Copies #554 WINE CELLAR RECORD BOOK	$32.50	@_____
_____Copies #641 POCKET ENCYCLOPEDIA OF CALIFORNIA WINES	$5.95	@_____
_____Copies #671 CORKSCREWS	$20.00	@_____
_____Copies #672 CALIFORNIA WINE DRINK BOOK	$4.95	@_____
_____Copies #673 WINE IN EVERYDAY COOKING	$5.95	@_____
_____Copies #542 WINE TOUR OF THE NAPA VALLEY	$4.95	@_____
_____Copies #543 WINE TOUR OF SONOMA/MENDOCINO	$4.95	@_____
_____Copies #544 WINE TOUR OF THE CENTRAL COAST	$4.95	@_____
_____Copies #676 VINTAGEWISE	$8.95	@_____
_____Copies #727 WINE LOVERS COOKBOOK	$7.95	@_____

Subtotal_____

California Residents 6% sales tax_____

plus $1.50 Shipping and handling (per order)____$1.50____

TOTAL Enclosed or charged to credit card_____

Please charge to my Mastercard of Visa card # _____

Expiration Date_____

Signature_____